MY EXPERIENCES IN
MODERN RETAIL

RAJENDRA K. ANEJA

Text copyright © 2017 Rajendra Kumar Aneja

All Rights Reserved

Dedicated to my late parents
Shri Hari Chand Aneja, and
Shrimati Prakash Kumari Aneja

And

My brother
Narendra Aneja

RETAIL PHILOSOPHY

"A Customer is the most important visitor on our premises. He is not dependent on us. We are dependent on him. He is not an interruption on our work. He is the purpose of it. He is not an outsider on our business. He is a part of it. We are not doing a favour by serving him. He is doing us a favour by giving us an opportunity to do so."

-Mahatma Gandhi

AUTHOR'S NOTE

This book presents a conceptual and practical framework for understanding Modern Retailing.

My work and travel in Unilever and Retail companies, over 45 years, took me to over 40 countries from Brazil all the way to Philippines, via Europe, Middle East, Africa, South Asia, etc. In all the countries that I visited, I keenly observed Retail concepts, stores, retail operations in a range of diverse products and buyer behaviour.

You will read about the critical success factors for managing a Retail business profitably. The book underscores the importance of Human Relations to be a successful Retailer. It also presents a case study of the Retail Industry in garments in Brazil. You will read about the Retail Revolution in developing countries and the future of the Malls and High Street shopping across countries.

The book covers how Indian retail is hoping to capture the market potential and the future of organised Retail in India. How Retailing will revolutionise lifestyles and values in rural India, is also covered. The intricacies and myths of modern fashion in Retail are also encompassed. It also discusses the characteristics of Entrepreneurial Managers in Retail.

This book also provides a checklist of 250+ points to be addressed, whilst building a new concept or retail store anywhere in the world.

This perspective of Modern Retail with detailed 'Nuts and Bolts' 250+ action points, is based on practical experiences and observations.

I thank my young colleagues Gnanesh Mehta, Rajesh Rajak, Amritaa Aneja and Deepa Rogye for their excellent contributions in collating this book. Gnanesh Mehta has also prepared a pithy and brilliant cover for the book. If you have any comments, please do write to me at rkaneja@anejamanagement.com.

ABOUT THE AUTHOR

RAJENDRA K. ANEJA

Rajendra Aneja is the Managing Director of a Management Consulting Company, providing services in Retailing, Marketing, Distribution, Feasibilities, Productivity, etc. He worked with Unilever for 28 years in India, Latin America and Africa. He worked in Unilever Brazil and as Managing Director of Unilever in Tanzania, Africa.

At Unilever he dealt with a diverse range of products and assignments. He has been involved in sales and marketing restructuring projects in Brazil, Colombia, Venezuela, Ecuador, Sri Lanka, etc.

Rajendra Aneja has also worked in Modern Retail in the Middle East, as the CEO of the large Sharaf Retail Group managing over 70 retail outlets in fashion, electronics and cosmetics, during which time the iconic Sharaf DG electronic concept was launched. 'Sharaf DG' is now rated as one of the Top 10 brands in the UAE.

Later he was CEO of Switz Group, a Foods manufacturing and retailing business across the Gulf. Aneja has also managed consulting assignments in Retail management in UAE, Kenya, Tanzania, Saudi Arabia, Brazil, etc.

Aneja has written widely on the evolution and future of Modern Retail in a number of prestigious Journals in India and abroad.

Aneja was a Sir Dorabji Tata Scholar throughout his graduation from Sydenham College of Commerce & Economics and also during his Masters Degree in Management Studies from Jamnalal Bajaj Institute in Mumbai. He was also a Government of India Scholar and received the Rotary Club Award for being the Best Student of the College. Subsequently he studied at the Harvard Business School and the Harvard Kennedy School of Government. He was invited to be a part of the Jury Panel for the Images Retail Awards, 2019, one of India's reputed Retail Awards.

He has written nine other books viz. "Conquer Rural Marketing Across Countries", "Business Express", "Surviving a Civil War", "Slices & Spices of Life: From Rio to Manila via Mumbai, Dubai, etc.", "A Common Man writes over One Thousand Letters to the Editor, Volume 1 & 2", "Agenda for a New India", "Little Thoughts for a Better World" and "Tiny Thoughts for a Bountiful Business".

APPRECIATIONS

"You write very well. Aim to write a book."

- **Mr. Khushwant Singh, Indian Writer**

"Human Relations in Retail Management is a crucial aspect which is often neglected. Your work is very relevant to India today."

Nihal Kaviratne CBE, Former Chairman, Unilever Indonesia. Currently Director Glaxo Pharma, India

"I hope you will not let this competitive world crush this talent of yours (writing), and will continue to write."

- **Mrs. Jaya Bhaduri Bachchan, Movie star**

"I read your article with interest. In writing it, you took on a tough assignment. You write very well. Many passages in the article are neatly phrased. The article compares favourably with the writing of professional journalists writing in India."

- **Mr. Rajinder Puri, Journalist, New Delhi**

CONTENTS

Section I

1	Retailing Revolution in Developing Countries	13
2	How to Manage a Retail Outlet Profitably?	19
3	Launching a New Retail Brand	29
4	Future Prospects of the Malls and High Street Shopping	33
5	Human Relations in Retail Management	43
6	Future of Organised Retail in India	64
7	Harvesting India's Rural Retail Potential	79
8	Wanted By Retail India: 'The Entrepreneurial Manager'	91
9	Is Indian Retail Floundering?	101
10	Retail Fashion: Magic and Myths	111
11	The A, B, C of Human Relations in Retail Management	118
12	Quotes and Discussions: Rajendra Aneja on Modern Retail	124

Section II

13	How to Start a New Retail Concept Store?The 'Nuts and Bolts'	138
14	Ready Reckoner: 'Nuts and Bolts'	209

PHOTOGRAPHS

Part I

1	High Street Shopping Will Continue To Be Popular, Boston (USA).	54
2	A Modern Retail Store for Fashion Garments in Lima, Peru.	54
3	A Modern Store for Footwear in Lima, Peru.	55
4	Supermarket Display Fruits and Vegetables, in Latin America.	55
5	Supermarkets' Clean Fruits and Vegetables, in Latin America.	56
6	Mobile Phones Area in a Modern Trade Electronics Outlet.	56
7	A Thriving Mall in Mumbai.	57
8	A View of an Upscale Mall in Mumbai.	57
9	An Elegant Fashion Mall in Sao Paulo, Brazil.	58
10	A Fashion Mall in Sao Paulo, Brazil.	58
11	Fashion Outlet at J. K. Shopping Mall in Sao Paulo, Brazil.	59
12	High Street Shopping Outlet at Rua Oscar Freire, Sao Paulo, Brazil.	59
13	Wholesale Markets for Garments in Jose Paulino, in Sao Paulo, Brazil.	60
14	Wholesale Markets for Garments in Braca, in Sao Paulo, Brazil.	60
15	Wholesale Markets for Garments in Jose Paulino, Sao Paulo.	61
16	A View of a Modern Store in Kingdom of Saudi Arabia.	61
17	Outlets in Wrentham Village, Massachusetts, United States.	62
18	Outlets in Wrentham Village, Massachusetts, United States.	62
19	The Iconic Sharaf DG Store in Dubai (UAE).	63
20	The Sharaf DG Store in Dubai: Amongst the Top 10 Brands, UAE.	63

Part II

21	High Street Shopping in Boston (USA).	133
22	High Street Shop, Boston (USA).	133
23	A Supermarket in Tanzania.	134
24	A Fashion Show in a Mall in Dubai.	134
25	An Attraction To Amuse Children in a Mall in the UAE.	135
26	Small Grocery Shops Modernise and Maintain High Levels of Hygiene, Abu Dhabi.	135
27	A Large Upscale Mall in Pune.	136
28	The Weekly Fiera Market in Sao Paulo, Brazil, Selling Local Handicrafts.	136
29	The Weekly Fiera Market in Sao Paulo, Brazil, Selling Brazilian Paintings.	137
30	The Weekly Fiera Market in Sao Paulo, Brazil, Refreshments for Shoppers.	137

SECTION I

1

RETAILING REVOLUTION IN DEVELOPING COUNTRIES

Sunita, a successful professional, resides with panache in a stylish apartment in posh Nariman Point, in Mumbai. Every Sunday, she drives her Mercedes for about 30 kilometers for over two hours. No, she is not participating in a car rally. She drives to shop in the glass and chrome, mushrooming malls in the suburbs of Mumbai. She buys her provisions and vegetables in the supermarkets. The cauliflower at Colaba vegetable market is no longer satisfactory.

Patricia works in a bank in Sao Paulo, Brazil. When she wants to buy a birthday present for her boyfriend, she spends six hours visiting elegant gift shops in Iguatemi or Morumbi Mall. Earlier, she would visit fashionable shops in tony Rua Oscar Freire.

Oscar Freire is Latin America's most prominent commercial street. It is also one of the best High Streets for shopping, in the world. The stylish tree-lined street stretches from Rua Alameda Branca to Rua Avenida Arnaldo in Jardins.

The brands located on Rua Oscar Freire and its sub-streets, include the world-famous Louis Vuitton, Armani, Dior, Montblanc (Sao Paulo has the highest number of Montblanc stores in the world), Cartier, Fendi, Kenzo, MaxMara,

MY EXPERIENCES IN MODERN RETAIL

Ermenegildo Zegna, Versace, Diesel, Cavalli, Bulgari, Salvatore Ferragamo, Custo Barcelona, Miss Sixty, Replay, and Tiffany & Co.. The street also houses the best of Brazilian fashion shops: Alexandre Herchcovitch, Forum, Ellus, NK Store, Sergio K, and Osklen.

Rua Oscar Freire is Brazil's 'luxury square'. Fashion stores in the street contributed to remove unsightly electrical poles and install underground fiber-optic lines, to make the street more enticing to shoppers. The shops are worried. Customers like Patricia, do not come anymore. Patricia prefers the malls.

In Dubai, malls are townships, complete with a dozen cinemas, five star hotels, and ice-skating rinks. They are a passionate way of life, alluring six million international tourists per annum. Millions of tourists' shop, dine and virtually live in the malls in Dubai. Malls in the Middle East are not built for shopping, but also for entertainment and fun. Builders are creating a few more million square meters of additional shopping space, in the next few years. The outlets in these malls get leased, before the ink on the construction drawings dries.

The way Patricia in Sao Paulo buys her gifts has undergone a major metamorphosis. Again, Sunita in Mumbai does not merely buy cauliflower. She is paying for style, and a new way of shopping. The generic value of products and brands matters, but how these are presented, sold and displayed, add meaning and value to the product. They also determine the sale of a particular brand.

A silent revolution in retailing is underway. Consumers are willing to spend hours travelling through clogged roads, pay more and splurge money on unbudgeted items via impulse buying, for a pleasurable shopping experience. Customers are often willing to spend, instead of saving. Five key variables are accelerating the change in shopping habits in developing countries, across the world.

1)   Higher disposable incomes:

We live in a richer world, a more affluent India and China. Generally, the middle and upper classes, across the world, are richer than they were, three decades ago. The middle classes in most developed and developing countries have been labouring for decades. Now, they have decent jobs, bank balances and homes. Their offspring, the 'computer generation' of our world, are born with the 'Can Do, Will Do,' mindset. The future belongs to them. The middle and affluent strata are willing to loosen their purse strings.

The enhancement in incomes and living standards is an international phenomenon. In India, the number of people living below the poverty lines dropped from over 50 per cent in 1972 to around 20 per cent now. Thus, about 300 million more consumers entered the lower middle class segment. They provide a sizeable market for all types of products, ready-made garments, packaged foods, household products, etc.

In Brazil, consumption of salt has augmented, indicating that more people are consuming three meals a day, providing a market for more consumer products. China's booming production machine has made its lower middle classes affluent. They are avid shoppers of fashion labels in Dubai's malls. They really, buy.

With more monies in the pockets, the educated and employed across the world, want to feel bright, look luminous, via fashionable apparel, cosmetics, facelifts and surgeries to slice

MY EXPERIENCES IN MODERN RETAIL

off the fat at the hips or thighs. Liposuction, anyone? Try Rio de Janeiro. Copacabana's sunny sands, breeze and doctors sculpt the best female forms.

2)   Convenience of one roof:

Let's go to a mall. There are over 1,500 shops to serve you, in clearly earmarked zones i.e. fashion, footwear, cosmetics, electronics, sports and kid's wear. There is an anchor supermarket, where Sunita buys her Italian pasta or Indian pickles, 'dals' and cheese from Holland. Hungry? There are a dozen restaurants to offer you cuisines, from Italy, Mexico and Lebanon. The world's food is at your footsteps now. The children are getting irritable? Rush to the kids' section. A range of games. Jaded? Twenty cinemas, with the latest blockbusters. Bored again? There is an ice-skating rink, in this mall, in the middle of a desert! There is also protected parking space for you. Hidden cameras record if anyone tries to steal the wipers of your car.

A shopping mall is designed for your family and you to have a range of conveniences, under a single roof. And, to lighten your wallet. Enjoy.

3)   Shopping: an exhilarating experience:

You visit a shopping mall, or a hypermarket, not just to buy a toothpaste or a TV. You can buy these items at many of the 10 million retail shops in India. A visit to a shopping mall or a hypermarket has to uplift your family and you. It is like seeing a great painting or a rare piece of art! This is not banter. The quantum of time energy and money spent in designing malls and supermarkets, their zones, outlets, defies imagination.

Each retailer tries to make his mall, supermarket or outlet, totally unique. The purchase of products is only a part of the shopping adventure.

The goal: to make your visit so gratifying and terrific that you visit the mall repeatedly.

4)   Globalisation of markets:

The fluidity of borders between countries has made it easier for products to travel. Reduction of import duties on items of everyday use like electronics, home decoration and personal care products, have provided wings to international brands. A mall in the Middle East offers all the brands marketed in the USA or Europe, frequently, at cheaper prices, due to lower duties. Certainly, the revolution in packaging materials over the last two decades have accelerated the globalisation of brands and their permeating far flung nation-markets. Mass-producing China has made the world its market, selling from a pin to a pillow to a piano. China has revolutionised the global supply-chain paradigm.

5)   Anti-incumbency vote:

The success of malls and supermarkets is also an anti-incumbency vote, against conventional 'bazaars' or 'souks' type of retailing. Shoppers just got glum with jumbled outlets, untidy streets or shops, price haggling, short weights and spurious products. Customers pay more for ambience, presentation, quality assurance, fun and surprises, as they shop.

MY EXPERIENCES IN MODERN RETAIL

These transformations in shopping habits are revolutionising retailing. The balance of power, as has happened in the USA and Europe, will shift, from manufacturers to retailers.

And, of course, Patricia and Sunita will reign as the Queens of the malls. They drive with a song in their hearts, 'Fleur-de-Lis' (whatever you desire).

2

HOW TO MANAGE A RETAIL OUTLET PROFITABLY?

11 Critical Success Factors

"Let us go to Mango," asserted Payel, as she, her husband Deepak and two sons got into their Mercedes, for shopping. "No," yelled 14-year-old Pallak, "I want to go to Marks & Spencer to buy jeans for my picnic!" "But," intervened the 10-year younger son Pulkit, "I want to bowl at the new mall!"

Deepak stopped the car. He proclaimed, "Well, make up your minds. I cannot drive in three directions!"

Deepak's dilemma is the predicament of global retailers and mall managers. They are staggered by the multifarious demands on their minds and facilities. Their challenge is how to cater ceaselessly to every whim of varying customers.

All the hype about the retailing explosion notwithstanding, for every one successful mall, there are four to five that are languishing in every city. Shoppers are capricious. They are really seeking experiences, not mere products. Thus, an exciting theme mall or a bargain always lures them. A decade ago all eyes in Dubai, were on Ibn Battuta Mall. Then customers waited breathlessly to enter Dubai Mall, one of the largest in the Middle East. In India, customers are anxious to savour the new shopping pleasures that retailers like Landmark and DLF propose to offer to them.

The 11 Critical Success Factors:

There are 11 fundamental factors, which determine the success of a mall or store.

1)   Site:

The most critical success factor in retailing is the location or the site. Ask anyone, the reason for the immense success of many crowded malls, like the Mall of Emirates in Dubai, the first reaction always is, "It is in the centre of the town!" The proximity of a mall and the ease of getting there is a critical determinant of where families shop. Smart retailers in the Middle East; do not hesitate to spend on building a public bridge, across the highway, just to facilitate ease of entry into their shopping malls. In most cities in developing countries, traffic is intense and roads are congested. So customers flock to malls, which do not entail inordinate driving.

In the mall shoppers tend to frequent the ground floor and first floor. The higher floors attract relatively less traffic, unless they have an alluring destination or concept store, e.g. a supermarket. Availability of escalators can augment the flow of shoppers to upper floors. Escalators should also be omnipresent at floor levels, for, the sheer size of malls can tire potential customers, especially senior citizens and children.

The site is particularly decisive for coffee shops and restaurants. Starbucks and Second Cup always choose corner sites, which lure customers.

2)   Parking:

Most malls tend to provide parking space from 1,000 to 6,000 cars, depending on the size. In Sao Paulo, new malls devote three to four floors of the mall to parking space. In retailing, every square foot can generate revenue, money and profit and so some malls neglect parking. If a shopper is going to be encumbered by having to hunt parking space, he may avoid visiting the mall.

Customers have to be mollycoddled. They are becoming choosy. They not only want ample, free parking, they literally want to walk from the parking area to the mall or their favourite retail outlet, within two to five minutes. Malls will have to pamper their customers in the future by providing these facilities and also offering valet services. The smart malls in the Middle East also offer limousine services to their customers, during peak hours when taxis are scarce.

3)   Product concept, merchandise:

Why should a customer visit a particular shop? What does the outlet have to offer? After all, a customer can buy a shirt, skirt, razor, electric iron and perfume in any of the millions of shops across the world. Why do consumers flock to Zara, Paris Gallery, Marks &Spencer, Virgin and H&M?

These stores offer concepts. They offer solutions, not merely a trouser or a handbag. They offer style, status and class. Some of them offer economy or value for money too. Principally, they offer a value proposition to every customer entering their outlet. Thus a clear concept, in the form of a value proposition, is crucial to the success of a retail store or mall. Customers have to be constantly indulged with new brands and experiences.

The signage of the store, layout, lighting and the music played inside, should supplement the concept. There is no tickle in playing loud Indian 'Bhangra' music in a store selling perfumes. Or, in playing soft, romantic Lebanese music in a grocery store.

The concept of a mall, 'pulls' and lures a certain characteristic crowd. Customers like to rub shoulders, with their own fraternity in terms of income, fashion and cultural patterns. People visit malls to also see other people! They want to feel cosy with co-shoppers. Customers, habituated to premium labels are not going to mix around with economy grocery shoppers.

So, if the mall is positioned at the top-end in fashion, like BurJuman in Dubai, or Morumbi in Sao Paulo, or Dhahran in Saudi Arabia, then proclaim it strongly in the advertising. In retail and fashion, it sometimes pays to be haughty!

The quality of merchandise offered is decisive in keeping consumers coming in repeatedly. Excellent quality, value for money, regular innovations and promotions lure customers. Innovation is the name of the retailing game. Creating constant excitement through regular updates of merchandise encourages the flow of traffic. It is vital to keep shoppers informed of new collections and merchandise at regular intervals.

4)   Customer service:

Successful stores have alert, energetic staff that is always willing to listen and help.

Walk into a fashion store, if the staff is sloppy, slovenly dressed, unavailable, you switch off mentally. If your trouser size is not available and the salesperson is unable to tell you when it will be available, you will be irritated. Such stores are in solemn trouble.

Virgin stores selling music are marvellous examples of fabulous customer service. Ask for a CD that is not available. They fill a form. Every week, you receive a call updating you. If they cannot get your CD in three to four weeks, they will telephone to apologise.

Many retail outlets across developing countries do not score well on customer service. Customers complain that they are not being 'attended to'. Their staff need training and development. They may have long working hours, inadequate breaks and meagre arrangements for refreshments. The working conditions for employees in many retail outlets need to be reviewed. Customer service is commendable, in Europe and the USA.

MY EXPERIENCES IN MODERN RETAIL

5) Visibility:

Customers believe what they see. Merchandise that is aesthetically displayed in an alluring manner draws shoppers. Merchandise that is dumped or shoddily kept in a store, may not move rapidly. Smart stores, devote space and time to the creation of show windows at vantage sites. They also deploy mannequins and shop-fitments to highlight stocks. Retailers employ professional architects, designers and visualisers to make the store appealing. The product must shout: "Take me home!!"

Zara is brilliant at displaying their products, via shelving and use of mannequins. Their stores have adequate stocks of every product and are yet never over-crowded with merchandise. Some retail outlets crowd inordinate merchandise in every corner. The store then appears like a discount warehouse rather than a stylish retail concept.

6) After sales service:

Every sale is a 'relationship' with a customer. The sale does not end with the cash memo bring printed. It begins. The sale is successful if the customer returns to the store. Thus, the staff should respect the customer even after the billing.

A refrigerator, which creates problems after delivery at home, requires immediate attention. The timing of the visit of the mechanic is important, as also his demeanour and dress. Many companies tend to sub-contract post sales technical service. The staff of the agencies visits homes at odd hours, without prior intimation, unshaved and shabbily attired. This damages the reputation of the manufacturing company, the brand and the store. The practice of outsourcing services to inept third parties to cut costs, causes loss of customers.

Stores should be very concerned about unhappy customers. Displease a customer once and you lose him or her forever. It is virtually impossible to woo back a peeved customer.

7) Customer loyalty programmes:

A sure way to build customer faithfulness is to have a loyalty programme, which offers incentives and gifts to consumers on achieving certain milestones. Customers who enrol in these loyalty programmes, thus, become an extended family of the store.

Customer loyalties can be enhanced through weekly or monthly newsletters about the various promotions in the stores. Some malls even publish monthly glossy journals, keeping loyal customers abreast of fashion trends.

Loyalty can also be nurtured by making customers feel secure in the mall or outlet. Malls, protected well by security cameras and watchmen, are favourites. However, excellent synchronisation with the local police and their cameras is essential. I saw a thief chased by the retail team at a premium outlet in Cape Town, South Africa. He fled from the mall into the street. The police arrested him within 30 minutes, since security cameras were tracking his entire escapade in and out of the mall.

8) Food and drinks, please!

Visits to shopping malls are becoming half to full day expeditions, due to inordinate transit times and parking delays. Moreover, in the mall itself, people tend to walk and walk and walk. So, they all feel thirsty and hungry. It is imperative to have a numerous outlets offering drinks and food to customers, at frequent intervals. Principally, a customer should not have to walk more than 10 minutes to get some refreshments.

Customers demand variety and fun in refreshments too. Food outlets should offer new concepts, menus and dishes, to lure customers. International cuisine has become local, in our times. Customers should be lured by a variety of international dishes, at malls. Food from Mexico, Italy or even Peru is chic!

Besides variety, customers are also demanding reasonable prices. They like varied product offerings but at economic prices. Malls have to segment the market, and offer ranges of foods i.e. the food courts, fine dining and the five-star concept restaurants. Food courts draw the bulk of shoppers, and should always be perky, with wholesome and economically priced food.

9) Customer help desks:

Malls are growing massive. Some of them are becoming small townships by themselves in the Middle East, South Africa and Latin America. Malls offer five-star hotel rooms, gymnasiums, shopping and restaurant facilities. Anyone can get lost in these five-seven star extravaganzas. Malls have to be user-friendly.

'Help Desks' offering maps, directions, etc. can facilitate the visits of customers. Staff who operates these desks should be friendly. It is important to have adequate number of staff at these Help Desks. There is little sense in building a premium mall and have customers waiting in a queue to locate the restroom.

The employees manning the Help Desks should ideally be multi-lingual and should be able to field queries in a few languages depending on the region.

Again having special events during festivals, etc., can draw more shoppers to the malls. With the proliferation of social media, consumers post their experiences almost immediately after an experience. This too can attract more footfalls.

10) Entertainment:

Retailers have to dance ceaselessly, to magnetise customers. Retail outlets will have sales, promotions, kids' competitions, music, pianists and violinists, to ensure customers flock to them. Malls organise carnivals, fashion shows, shopping festivals to ensure customers patronise them. Children are a major influence in determining the choice of the retail outlet to be visited. So, they have to be lured with games, sports, magic shows, face painting, competitions, etc.

Malls are adding ice-rinks, hotels, massage parlours, beauty salons, theatres, movies, music shows to their premises, to ensure they keep customers enthralled. The onus is on the mall to provide shopping options and entertainment activities, to keep the entire family tantalised.

11) Ringing cash register: Melodious music!

The variables affecting the success of a store or mall are equally important. A fashion store cannot be scintillating in visibility, but have shoddy salesmanship. Nor can an electronics store be excellent in after sales service, but not offer the latest models of washing machines.

These 11 variables must blend harmoniously to woo consumers, and keep them returning insistently, to the mall or the store. The various factors must interweave, just as in an orchestra, music from all the instruments has to blend to make harmonious music. For the successful retailer, ringing cash registers make the most melodious music!

3
LAUNCHING A NEW RETAIL BRAND

At a press conference, Winston Churchill was asked, "Who is the greatest Socialist in history?" Without blinking an eye, Churchill replied, "Christopher Columbus!" When the stunned audience asked, why, Churchill replied, "When he started his journey, he did not know where he was going; when he reached his destination, he did not know that he had reached."

Retailers who launch new brands, without clear goals and strategies, are like socialists described by Winston Churchill! Hence it is important to understand how to launch a new retail brand, be it a store selling shirts or refrigerators or lipsticks.

In the tough retail scenario, which prevails globally, launching a new retail brand is an arduous undertaking. It is an expensive proposition and can cost millions of dollars. Hence rigorous homework is crucial.

1) First parameter - Anvil of Four Ps of marketing:

The first parameter of launching a new retail product is to be audit the launch package on the anvil of the Four P's of marketing i.e. Product, Price, Place and Promotion.

a) Product: The retailer must think through the product to be launched, its value proposition, the positioning, its ingredients, segment of consumers being catered to and the packaging or appearance of the store. Since the retail outlet, from where the product will be sold, is a very integral part of the product, its conceptualisation and architecture, is an essential part of the product design itself.

b) Price: The retailer must deliberate whether the Pricing of the product will be at premium, popular or discount levels. Pricing will also be determined by the positioning in the market. Competitor prices will also impact the pricing strategy.

c) Place: Next, the retailer has to decide, how and where the product will be distributed and sold. Should the product be sold in top-class malls? Or, should it be sold in the High Street outlets?

d) Promotions: Finally, marketers have to decide the type of Promotions that will be used to promote the product. This covers advertising the product via media like the television, radio, newspapers, magazines, etc. It also embraces other Promotions like in-shop activities, sampling, etc., to entice usage and frequent buying of the product.

2) Second parameter - Top class team:

The second key parameter in launching a successful new retail brand is to select a top-class, competent team to launch the product concept and the store. Every retailer should focus on building and buying the best team, that his budget permits him to do so. Many new retail concepts and brands fail to deliver, because the entrepreneur has scrounged on building a high-class team.

Good professionals cost more, but they deliver success. The quality of people, their commitment, dedication and enthusiasm are critical variables in determining the success of the new retail brand. Brilliant quality professionals do more than they are required to do in a product launch. They walk the extra mile, work the extra night, think of one extra brand feature, which can be crucial in winning in a fiercely competitive market.

3) Third parameter - New paradigms:

The third key parameter in launching a new retail brand, is to think outside the box or normal paradigms. For instance, most retailers in developing countries, when launching a new product, think only in terms of malls and High Streets. However, in the largest markets of the world like China, India and Brazil, rural markets and slums house 20 to 30 per cent of the populations. The disposable incomes of these segments are growing and lifestyles are modernising rapidly. Retailers have to evolve retail mechanics to reach these consumers also.

Retailers launching new products should read evolving markets rapidly, to comprehend new trends, patterns and fashions in the marketplace.

4) Last point, clear, quantifiable goals:

It is crucial to determine clear goals for at least three to five years prior to launching a new retail brand. These goals should be quantified metrics; not mere generalised statements. Some of the metrics that can be used for defining the goals of a new launch are: 1) Market share, 2) Profit contribution, 3) Sales turnover and 4) Volumes in quantity terms.

Specific quantifiable goals help in channelling the right level of investments in the brand being launched. They also contribute towards objective assessment of the store concept, product performance and of the team working on the brand.

Abraham Lincoln, once asserted, "What is the use of running, if you are on the wrong road?" In politics, as well as in launching a new retail brand, it is crucial to be crystal clear about the strategic and financial results to be achieved.

Summary:

In summary, smart retailers when launching new brands will ensure that they audit the entire marketing package on the anvil of the Four Ps of marketing, recruit the best teams that money can buy, recognise emerging consumer segments and have quantifiable goals for at least five years

The communication goals of the new brand should be simple and clear. This is best illustrated by this story of a rural farmer Jaganathan. He ran a chicken farm on a rural highway. However, the traffic was so heavy that 25 chickens were being run over every day. He called the Mayor and complained. The Mayor, had the workers erect a sign: "Slow: School crossing."

Three days later Jaganathan told the mayor that cars were yet speeding. Another sign pronounced: "Slow: Children playing."

However, motorists continued to speed. Chickens continued to die. Jaganathan, put up his own sign. A week later, the mayor surprised by the silence, went over to check the sign put up. He was astounded. It read, "Nudist colony: Watch the chicks". Every motorist was slowing down!

This is effective communication. Good retailers, like this farmer, learn to think creatively!

4

FUTURE PROSPECTS OF THE MALLS AND HIGH STREET SHOPPING

The permeation of the mall culture will have a fundamental impact on High Street shopping. High Street is a typical British phrase, meaning the main commercial and retail street in the town. In the large cities, each neighbourhood may have its own High Street.

Even villages in Britain have a High Street. Typically, it would house the post office, mailbox, a public pay phone and the grocery or convenience outlet. However, the High Street of a town may not be christened 'High Street' officially, and a street actually named 'High Street', may not be the retail or commercial artery of the town. High Street Kensington, is not the fashion or shopping hub of London, but is yet named as such. The Americans describe their shopping and commercial artery as a Main Street.

Before the emergence of the malls in India, shoppers flocked to High Streets like South Extension in Delhi, or Colaba in Mumbai, Regent or Oxford Street in London to buy their fashionable suits and skirts.

High Streets are the results of evolution of consumer marketing. They were not really planned. They evolved with time. There was no grand plan that Connaught Circus in Delhi or Colaba in Mumbai would become alluring shopping zones or streets. These markets evolved as flocks of richer customers gravitated towards these residential localities and shopkeepers had to meet their stylish requirements. Bandra was a sleepy suburb of erstwhile 'Bombay', 40 years ago. Now, it leads the retail fashion revolution in Mumbai.

Compared to the haphazard evolution of High Street markets, mall managers, sweat blood, to ensure the balance between outlets of different merchandise. High Streets provide the bustle and thrill of shopping in a variety of stores. However, lately they have been losing their lustre and clientele to the malls.

Why High Streets Are Losing Their Luster?

1)   Unorganised, chaotic!

Since High Streets evolve with time, there is no specific pattern in their layout. A tailor could be located next to a branded apparel shop or a footwear outlet next to a restaurant. Since the owner of each building or shop is free to negotiate with each outlet, there is no pattern in the composition of the retail outlets. Sometimes there could be an interesting assortment of outlets, as in Colaba causeway. Nevertheless, there could also be a dozen outlets selling the same or similar products, because the first was a success, for instance, the row of over dozen outlets selling branded luggage, at the street along Lal Bagh in Lower Parel in Mumbai.

2)   Parking: what is that?

The biggest threat to High Street shopping is quite simply, absence of parking space. Most urban middle class families now own a minimum of two cars. We have forgotten to walk.

Therefore, there is massive pressure on parking space on the roads. A High Street shopping area anywhere in the world, if it is really worth visiting, has really no space for parking cars. So, shoppers have to park their cars, a few kilometers away, and then either taxi to the shops or walk down there. The issue is more complex on the return journey, when the shoppers are laden with bags.

3)   Poor to weak security:

High Street shopping is also being endangered by security concerns in some cities and countries. There is a higher possibility of pickpockets operating in the streets, than in shopping malls. Police officers do protect the High Streets, but malls have elaborate security personnel, systems and cameras. Says Rakhir, who works as the sales manager of a 5-star hotel in Delhi, "I feel very safe and secure in the shopping malls. When I shop in the streets, I always felt stared at by guys. I am most uncomfortable!"

4)   Where are the food and the games?

Shopping is increasingly becoming a family activity, involving all members. High Streets offer a circumscribed range of options for the entire family. In a mall, mummy could be shopping, the young children could be at play center, the teenagers could walk into a movie and papa could just sip coffee. The High Street does not offer these varied options to the entire family. The availability of an assortment of services and temptations for everyone in the family, is a unique offering of the malls. Large malls often have 5-star hotels as an attachment. For instance, Stanton in Johannesburg in South Africa, Dubai Mall and Mall of Emirates in Dubai are all linked to hotels. The presence of hotels in the vicinity of the malls ensures that shoppers have additional restaurant options. Moreover, tourists staying in the hotels also have easy access to the malls.

5)   Do not forget the basics!

Try finding a toilet after a few hours of shopping, in Oxford Street in London. The best chance is to visit a McDonald's. Or, if you are weary of walking in the shops at Rua Bela Cintra in Sao Paulo, try to find a bench to rest your legs. Again, your best bet would be a bar or a coffee shop. High Streets do not have as many toilets, resting places or coffee shops, as do the new malls.

High Street Food yet Reigns!

Significantly, High Streets offering food, have traditionally managed to neutralise the onslaught of malls and food courts. The range of open-air cafes and restaurants at Al Diyafa in Dubai, allures hundreds of families every evening. The restaurants opposite BurJuman Centre, Dubai, attract customers every hour, despite the presence of food courts in proximately located elegant malls.

Similarly, the Pandara Road and Moti Mahal restaurants, yet entice visitors to Delhi. The daily crowds yet swell at Madras Cafe and Mysore Cafe at Matunga or Visawa in Dadar in Mumbai. These eateries have and will survive the onslaught of food courts in the malls.

It Is All in the Rentals, Really!!

The tussle of deciding whether to set up a concept in a mall or the High Street, will depend significantly on the rentals in these areas and the expected revenues per square foot. If the rentals in the malls are very high, retailers will be compelled to move to the High Street, where rentals may be modest. Strong and premium brands like 'Rolex' or 'Armani' could do equally well in a mall or the 'High Street'. However, if the brand is nascent in a country, the rentals per square foot and the actual space rented, will determine the commercial viability.

Rentals for mall space can range widely on a per square foot basis in the malls in Dubai, depending on the size and location of the outlet. High Street rentals would depend on the locality and the location, but principally would be lower than the malls. The high rentals in India in the premium locations could continue for some more time due to the desire to recover costs expeditiously.

Competition Improves the High Streets:

High–street shopping will have to budget simple facilities like resting benches for their shoppers and restrooms, in case they wish to compete with the malls in the future. The competition from shopping malls will certainly spur High Street outlets, to improved presentation and modernisation of their outlets. Consider for instance, the rebirth of the 'Heera-Panna' shopping zone in Mumbai. For decades, it had been a haven for shoppers for electronics, premium crockery, household and personal items. Then, a few steps away, Mumbai's first shopping mall, 'Crossroads' emerged in shining glory. Immediately the outlets at 'Heera-Panna' went through a facelift, with enhanced claddings, billboards, product offerings, parking facilities, etc.

Similarly, the outlets in Delhi's prestigious High Street South Extension market, have consistently improved their facades and offerings to foster repeat visits. Competition does spur superior performance.

The malls will offer a range of services, which the High Streets will find it difficult to match, in the short run. For instance, the Al Futtaim City Centre Mall, even in Muscat, (population less than a million), offers its shoppers about 150 fashion and contemporary retail outlets. However, to make the shoppers comfortable, the mall offers wheelchairs to the elderly and infirm at no extra cost, complimentary baby carts, pay phones, an Information Desk, Mall gift vouchers of required denominations, etc.

The mall further offers separate prayer rooms for men and women, baby changing rooms, restrooms across the mall, special restrooms for the disabled, ATM booths of five banks, with one bank offering full-fledged banking services, multi-level parking for 2,250 cars and regular taxi services. It also offers valet services.

The mall also offers a Lost and Found service, security, easy access flyover, currency exchange services and even a Post Box facility. In addition, whilst the Mall closes at 10 p.m. daily, the anchor store Carrefour is open until midnight daily to facilitate shopping. There are coordinated promotions like sales, children contests, etc. In addition, since the summer sun heats the day to 50 degrees Celsius, the parking lots are all covered, so that the car is not a baking oven, when the shopper returns.

The Dubai Mall in the UAE has raised the expectations of consumers even further, with all its facilities. The site area was in excess of 12.1 million square feet. The structural steel used in the mall, was double than that deployed in the Eiffel Tower, i.e. 7,300 tonnes. The net leasable area is equal to area of 50 football fields, strung together. The mall houses around 1,200 retail outlets. It has a gold market with 220 retailers. It has the world's largest indoor aquarium, with 33,000 living animals including sharks. A tunnel runs through the tank, holding 10 million liters of water. There is parking for 14,000 cars and a five-star hotel with 700 rooms.

Now, how can any High Street compete with this mall, which is a town by itself? A visitor to Dubai can stay in the hotel next to the mall and just stay put there, since all the holiday facilities are available at the mall.

Thus, the emergence of such malls and big-box category killers will certainly dampen sales of the smaller outlets in the High Streets.

The emergence of large electronics retailers like 'Croma' and 'Vijay sales' in vantage locations in Mumbai city and many malls in other towns, would have impacted the smaller players. The emergence of professional electronics retailers like 'Jumbo', 'Plug Ins', etc., has impacted other electronics players at Al Fahidi Street in Dubai.

Brazil has exclusive malls for sales of furniture. Dubai has 1,00,000 square feet electronics outlets. Saudi Arabia has exclusive 50,000 square feet outlets selling only books and stationery.

High Street shopping will also flourish, depending on the products being sold, the status attached to the street and the segment of the market being catered to. There will be co-existence, perhaps even some congruence, between the malls and High Street shopping in the future.

1)   High streets improvements:

The arrival of mall culture will definitely depress some sales in the High Streets. High Street outlets will have to spruce and energise themselves to meet the sharper competition from the malls. Grocery stores in Bangalore were the first to improve their appearances and presentations, as early as the mid-1995s, to cater to the more discerning consumers in the city.

The mall culture will also improve customer service in the High Street. The competition from malls will kindle better service at street outlets too.

2)   High Streets must think laterally!!

Lateral thinking, generating unique new paradigms, could benefit High Street retailers. For instance: No visit to London is complete without a walk on Oxford street, i.e. from Marble Arch to Oxford Circus stations. Many popular fashion brands are housed in this High Street, between these two metro rail stations, including Selfridges and John Lewis. In the next few decades, the malls may lure sizeable customers away from this crowded pilgrimage street. So why not think of a totally innovative solution of a transparent glass roof, covering the entire street, banning all traffic on the road, and transforming it into a mall? Yes, make a few changes: provide play areas, air-conditioning and heating, etc. Then, you could have a ready-made fashion mall!

a) Prisons of Fortaleza and Salvador in Brazil: In towns like Fortaleza and Salvador in Brazil, if you need to buy local handicrafts, paintings, embroidered tablecloths, laced dresses, etc., you normally visit a single storied building, in a compound. Each outlet is installed in a single room-type shop. Each shop leads into another. I was so intrigued by these cute markets that I enquired of my colleagues, how these evolve. The reply flummoxed me. These building were prisons many years ago!

As crime rates declined, the prisons were no longer required. The authorities converted these prisons into markets for art and handicrafts! Each shop in a room had earlier been a cell for prisoners. This is a brilliant example of an exquisite mall, with elegant products and shops, metamorphosing out of prison building. Thus, necessity is the mother of all invention and opportunities for retail are boundless. We merely have to spot them and build on them.

b) High Street 'market-malls' in Montevideo, Uruguay: In Montevideo, the capital of Uruguay, some of the street markets, are already clustered in predesigned format and have transparent dome-like circular ceilings, which give them an appearance of being malls. These High Street 'market-malls', will never be threatened by any retail concept. Youngsters flock here every night to sip champagne and beer till the wee hours of the morning.

High Street cluster of outlets must also acquire some snob value, to generate and retain their clientele. It does matter socially to have bought your suit from Regent Street, Chelsea or Savile Row.

3) Diversification in to new markets:

The preponderance of malls or specialised retail concepts can also lead to a changed sales and marketing strategy amongst High Street retail outlets. A decade ago anyone in Dubai, who wanted to buy a laptop or a desktop computer, headed straight to Computer Street. However, the arrival of electronics retailers like 'Jumbo', 'Plug Ins', etc., changed the computer market paradigm in Dubai.

Now consumers want to buy their laptops and accessories from retailers who display the products alluringly, explicate the technical features, and advise which brand or model to buy. The emergence of a mall, i.e. 'Al Ain Centre', specialising in computers and accessories, also impacted sales in the 'Computer Street'. The retailers in 'Computer Street', felt the pinch of loss of consumers. They have diversified into exports to African and other Middle East countries. Now, they flourish.

4) More Elegance please!

In the current phase of developing shopping malls, we should aim to build theme malls, which are exquisite and architecturally innovative, so that shopping in them is a real delight. A classic example of themed mall concept is the Ibn Battuta Mall on the Sheikh Zayed Road of Dubai.

So, let us also build for joy and beauty.

5
HUMAN RELATIONS IN RETAIL MANAGEMENT

The principal challenge confronting Indian retailers in the coming decade will be to staff their operations and motivate their teams. The challenge is accentuated by the expansion of retailing in India. There is an acute paucity of adequate numbers of trained retailers. The paucity of formal retailing education in India further exacerbates the problem of recruiting knowledgeable personnel rapidly.

The shopping and retailing patterns in India are undergoing a profound change. Earlier urban Indian was content to shop in small grocery stores. The new generation Indian wants to buy trousers and perfumes, in swanky shopping malls.

The introduction of modern large-scale retail formats in the rural areas will metamorphose the villages of this country, in a breath-taking manner. Imagine, formats of 1,00,000 square feet selling agricultural equipment and computers in the villages in Punjab and Uttar Pradesh. Rural India, which was so destitute two decades ago, that even a bar of soap, was cut into small pieces and sold, for as low as 50 paise, is now ready for agricultural supermarkets.

India's mood in the urban and the rural areas, can lucidly be summed as: Good-bye Socialism, Welcome 'Sonyism'!

MY EXPERIENCES IN MODERN RETAIL

The immediate issue confronting Indian retailers is how to recruit large numbers of employees in the next two to three years, train the new entrants, keep them motivated and imbibe a culture of delivery amongst them. 'Business is people' and managing people and motivating them is a crucial building block in expediting Modern Retail formats.

The 10 Critical Success Factors for Great Human Relations Management:

1)   Build corporate passion:

The first ingredient of flourishing human relations in retail management is to imbibe a passion for success amongst the employees. If the staff members are the direct employees of the company, there will be greater commitment and unity of purpose. Personnel sourced from external agencies, will be more dedicated to their primary employers, but every effort should be made to involve them fully. Staff should be enthused by the corporate mission. Organisations succeed, not merely when the directors are motivated, but when every employee down the line, i.e. the packer or the security guard, are fully charged by the same mission.

Passion is a vital ingredient for success in any venture, more so in retailing. Smart retailers focus on building service oriented organisations, with steady profits flowing in.

Walmart has built a rock-solid loyal team, with missionary zeal. They even sing and clap together, in the mornings daily before commencing work in the supermarkets.

2) Stock options to all:

Retailers would do well to make every employee a partner, through stock options or a profit sharing scheme. It would be provident to evolve a scheme to place the entire team, including the packing man, on a salary and stock options remuneration system. A watchman, who knows that he has a stake in the final profits, in the form of a bonus or a stock option, will ensure zero levels of shrinkage or pilfering.

Employees are the assets of any business. Employees have brains, ideas and intelligence. However, some of them may have lacked the opportunity to develop as much as others. Hence a good business will respect even the lowest rung employee.

Principally, it is best for a retail company to have own teams for sales, merchandising and customer service. A company's own employees, are more passionate about its mission, goals and values. Recruiting a dedicated company team may cost more than outsourcing, but in the long run, the retail outlet can become an institution and not remain just a shop.

Talented retail employees and managers are tough to recruit. A decade ago, companies use to display boards, 'Trespassers will be prosecuted'. Now the boards read, 'Trespassers will be recruited!!' Such is the shortage of talent and skill in the retail sector.

There are also strong possibilities of picking up excellent quality retail managers from South East Asia and the Middle East due to their experience in the Modern trade.

Global recruitment firms and local head-hunters can play a pivotal role in identifying suitable talent in concerned countries. Personal networking can also help to identify quality managers.

Using reputed recruitment firms can accelerate recruitment of front line staff. This issue is not very complicated in India, for the staff is principally recruited from within the country. The recruitment of employees in the Middle East is more complex, because they have to be recruited from a dozen countries like Philippines, Jordan, Syria and Russia, etc.

3)   Unionisation:

Unions are a reality and should be welcomed. They are the collective voice of the employees, the partners in the enterprise.

Unions are constructive when the relationships between the employers and employees are fair. It is best to treat their workers humanely and fairly.

4)   The basics:

Retailing is a hard and tough business. It is also rigorous. The floor staff stands on their feet for about eight hours per day. They deal with polite and sensible customers. They also manage crazy and schizophrenic customers. The job of the salesperson on the floor is not merely physically exacting, but is also emotionally draining.

Retailing is becoming fiercely competitive, simply because of the abundance of brands flooding the market, in all arenas e.g. fashion, footwear, homes, food, etc. Retailers have tough norms requiring every store to have a date bound profit plan. Store managers will have to play the role of entrepreneurs and businessmen and not mere store guardians.

Changing existing mind-sets and motivating personnel will also require ensuring basic hygiene factors to all personnel. It is crucial to provide restrooms, canteens, dining areas and recreation rooms to the staff. A retailer will earn a lot of revenue per square foot, when those who are responsible for generating it are well treated.

In retailing the front line, is the last line. The sales boy or girl, interacting with the customer on the floor, makes the sale or blights it.

Marks & Spencer, one of the leading retailers of the world, do not make anything themselves. They outsource the manufacture of their entire merchandise. However, when their managers go to appoint a new company as suppliers, they check the facilities for the staff.

Then they survey the kitchens and dining areas, where the employees of that vendor eat. If they are satisfied with the quality and hygiene of the vendor's premises, only then they engage in a dialogue for supplies.

The philosophy of Marks and Spencer that if the staff of our suppliers can rest and eat well we will get better quality merchandise, is very sensible indeed.

If the staff of a retail outlet has to wait in the queue to visit the toilet, they will certainly keep customers waiting at the till. So, a smart retailer will care and share his success with the team.

5) Respect the sales floors:

The profits of retail outlets are generated on the floors of the store, through the sales of the products. However, it is the sales employees who actually sell the products and convert them into cash.

An astute retailer will walk the floors of the store every day. In a customer service oriented retail outlet, the supervisory staff, whether managers or directors or the chairman of the company, will walk the floors. They will talk to the staff, about their families, their health, transport facilities and only then about their products. They will seek advice, views and customer responses, from their floor sales staff.

Senior managers should talk to the staff. Speak to the customers. Make friends with them. And smile. A smile is free and is yet priceless.

The best retailer of our times, Mr. Sam Walton said, "Our best ideas come from the shop floors." He spent hours daily, talking to his staff and customers on shop floors.

CEOs should focus on organisation or institution building, knowing their customers and talking to floor staff.

The CEO sets the tone, style and character of the company, more so, in retail organisations where visibility is high, since the store is the primary brand being marketed. The style and conduct of the CEO percolates down the line, to the shop floors.

Operating managers in merchandising, marketing, visuals, etc. should also be required to spend some time every week on the floors, studying the movement of merchandise, talking to floor employees and even getting feedback from customers. Customers in stores, love talking and giving opinions.

6) Do not forget grooming!!

The sale in retailing takes place, when the customer sees and likes a product and talks to the salesperson. That is the ignition key turning in the car, the magic moment. Hence, the presentation of the product and salesperson are crucial.

Retailing is about the staff donning clean and well-pressed uniforms. It is about shaving daily. It is about using the right type and quantum of deodorant. Retailing is also about bright enthusiastic eyes and warm smiles. It is about polished shoes. These are fundamental factors, but they make or break a sale.

These hygiene factors have organisational implications. How many sets of uniforms should be given to a staff member? A retailer gives only two blouses to the sales ladies, over a period of six months. So, should the girl be washing/pressing her blouse every night, after she reaches home at 11 pm, after having stood on the shop floors for nine hours?

All these issues underscore the need for manuals, defining every operation of the store. It would clarify timings, responsibilities, operating conditions, policy on uniforms, leaves, breaks, pilferage, shrinkages, etc. Retailers like Woolworth and Marks & Spencer have comprehensive operating manuals, which delineate operations and working conditions.

Again, should the retail store, provide deodorants, hair trimming service, shoe polish facilities at the store itself? If left to the employee, he may neglect them, when he is running to catch a metro train or a bus in the morning.

Many five-star hotels have mandatory showering services, as soon as any employee walks in through the staff door.

Fashion retailing, in terms of service, is akin to the five-star hotel business. It is useful to recruit the grooming and communications staff from top star hotels whilst training retail staff. Whilst building a new electronics chain, a top business group in the Middle East recruited a grooming manager of a star category hotel. This manager spent all her time on the shop floors, counselling the floor staff on personal cleanliness, greeting and managing customers.

7) Ceaseless training and development:

One of the best investments a retail group can make is to recruit the best retail trainers in the industry. The investment pays for itself. The trainer should develop an annual training calendar, for all employees involved in operations.

In a well-managed retail organisation each employee would spend at least 10 working days per annum, in classroom training. Training has to be constant and ceaseless, in the classroom and above all, on the floors on a daily ongoing basis.

Retail organisations, which focus seriously on training and development, have highly motivated employees. Employees are always grateful to companies, which fortify their skills and conceptual prowess.

Retail groups selling products like farm implements and seeds, etc., in the rural areas, will have to ensure that the staff selected in the urban areas, is given suitable rural orientation, prior to being posted to the smaller towns or rural areas.

The retail explosion in India has major ramifications for retail academic training in India. There are still few retail institutes, providing academic lessons and practical training in retail to youngsters. The business schools have to focus seriously on a new Master's degree in Retail Management. The Retail Academy managed by the Pearl Group in Delhi is an excellent initiative in strengthening retail education in India.

8) Do not lose your people!!

India has a population of about 1.3 billion. The world has around seven billion people. Yet, recruiters lament, they are unable to source a CEO, an accountant or even a brand manager.

Talent and skill are scarce. It is always sensible to retain quality staff. It takes decades, to inculcate the team with corporate values and a certain 'way of doing business'. It tests nerves to train managers. Then, to lose them in a flash of anger, or whim or a competitive lure of some more money, is avoidable.

Andrew Carnegie, the steel billionaire of the USA asserted, "Take away my factories and my buildings, take away my products, but leave behind my salesmen, and in one year's time, I will be back to where I left off."

The people, who work in the store, are the jewels of the company. A smart retailer will value his human resources.

It is wise practice to recruit 10 to 15 per cent extra personnel, so that sudden departures, do not have adverse impacts on the operations.

Smart retailers retain their staff, via motivation and pride of achievement. Recognising the Best Salesperson, the Best Store, highest Growth rates, Best Store Manager, Most Profitable Store, Star Performers Club, awarding Team prizes, trophies, etc., can build team spirit and motivation.

Experience proves, happy teams, generate profits. A store may make continuous losses for five to six years sometimes, but with right leadership and motivation they start churning profits.

A retail group in Bahrain, after three years of excellent profits, found the bottom line flagging. The management appointed a new CEO, who sacked three of the 10store managers, in two weeks. The morale plummeted. Everyone went to the office, expecting to be sacked. Another three store managers quit. The company needed six new store managers. They could not recruit managers from the market, because the word was out on the street, that the Human Resource (HR) policies of the company are fickle. Finally, after 10 months, the company was able to recruit six candidates, at double the remuneration. However, sales had plunged by 40 per cent. Such situations are preventable.

Smart retailers welcome automation of routine tasks. Instance: security personnel are normally entrusted with calibrating footfalls. However electronic machines, installed at the entrance of stores can also compute the footfalls, reducing the level of human error.

9) Building careers:

It is vital to build careers and promote people from within the company. Internal progression systems augment loyalty and boost morale. The staff is strongly motivated by the belief that they will grow, when they deliver results.

There should be a well-defined succession plan in the company and potential candidates should be identified and groomed with adequate training and exposures.

10) Dance sometimes:

Working in any company should be fun and rejuvenating. The staff should look forward eagerly to coming to work daily. This is possible, when the team also spends informal times together. The staff of a retail store should have fun celebrating birthdays, marriage anniversaries, picnicking, rejoicing and dancing together.

The management of the store, even the Chairman or CEO should join in these fiestas to build team spirit. The carnival in Brazil is a splendid example of collective celebration and rejoicing, which bonds people of all classes and levels together, for 10 days of sustained fun.

Winning is exciting, becoming rich is glorious and it is vital to celebrate success together. If the employees of a retail company dance, sing, eat and rejoice together, the company stays together.

As, Mother Teresa said, "A family which eats together, stays together!!"

PHOTOGRAPHS, PART I

Photograph 1: High Street shopping will continue to be popular, Boston (USA).

Photograph 2: A Modern Retail store for fashion garments in Lima, Peru.

Photograph 3: A Modern store for footwear in Lima, Peru.

Photograph 4: Supermarket display fruits and vegetables, in Latin America.

Photograph 5: Supermarkets' clean fruits and vegetables, in Latin America.

Photograph 6: Mobile phones area in a Modern Trade electronics outlet, India.

Photograph 7: A thriving mall in Mumbai, India.

Photograph 8: A view of an upscale mall in Mumbai, India.

Photograph 9: An elegant Fashion Mall in Sao Paulo, Brazil.

Photograph 10: A Fashion mall in Sao Paulo, Brazil.

Photograph 11: Fashion outlet at J. K. Shopping mall in Sao Paulo, Brazil.

Photograph 12: High Street shopping outlet at Rua Oscar Freire, Sao Paulo, Brazil. It is one of the top fashion streets in the world.

MY EXPERIENCES IN MODERN RETAIL

Photograph 13: Wholesale markets for garments in Jose Paulino, in Sao Paulo, Brazil.

Photograph 14: Wholesale markets for garments in Braca, in Sao Paulo, Brazil.

Photograph 15: Wholesale markets for garments in Jose Paulino, in Sao Paulo, Brazil.

Photograph 16: A view of a Modern store in Kingdom of Saudi Arabia.

MY EXPERIENCES IN MODERN RETAIL

Photograph 17: Outlets in Wrentham Village, Massachusetts, United States.

Photograph 18: Outlets in Wrentham Village, Massachusetts, United States.

Photograph 19: The iconic Sharaf DG store in Dubai (UAE).

Photograph 20: The iconic Sharaf DG store in Dubai (UAE). The Store is amongst the Top 10 Brands in the country.

6
FUTURE OF ORGANISED RETAIL IN INDIA

India should foster Modern Trade for the economic value that it adds to the economy, the employment it would generate and the improved quality of customer offerings. Modern retailing as exemplified through supermarkets and hypermarkets is an imminent phase in India. We should facilitate it.

If a country like India with a population of over a billion encourages the Modern Trade, it will have an explosive impact in terms of creating employment and payment of taxes. Modern Trade will also improve service to consumers.

Supermarkets being in the organised and visible sector pay taxes diligently. Moreover, being larger in size, they are governed by labour laws.

Modern stores generate many jobs. Walmart is one of the largest employers in the whole world. An average grocery supermarket model shop generates about five to seven jobs per store of 1,000 square feet. For every such job created, there are about seven times jobs created indirectly i.e. transporters, drivers, loaders, watchmen, etc. Thus, for every 1,000 square feet of retail space created, about 35 new jobs would be generated in the economy. So a store of 50,000 square feet could generate about 2,500 jobs. India could easily do with about 10,000 such stores, thus creating millions of jobs. And this could happen very rapidly.

Consumers are assured of good quality products, because hypermarkets clean and grade their wares like fruits and vegetables to merchandise them. In many developing countries, fruits and vegetables are frequently sold on open pavements and are often coated with dust.

Supermarkets offer better prices to the consumers. They buy in bulk, and are able to negotiate better prices from the farmers and suppliers. Since the market is very competitive, such savings are normally passed on to consumers.

Staff who work in hypermarkets and supermarkets undergo regular training and development, which enhances their skills. If the staff working in such stores perform well, they can have careers in retailing i.e. literally graduate from floor salesmen to managers.

As supermarkets and retailers grow, they also follow socially responsible policies. Marks & Spencer follow very sensible policies. When they select a new supplier, they first check the facilities for the staff. Only if the supplier clears this critical test, they proceed further to foster a relationship with the vendor.

Enlightened retailers and supermarkets become partners with their vendors. They collaborate to improve the basic product itself. For instance, the McDonald's research centre works with farmers, to improve the quality of the potatoes they use for their French fries.

Positive Approach Needed:

We should refrain from politicising the arrival of organised retail. Even Russia and China have principally turned fashionably capitalist and welcomed hypermarkets and Western brands with musical bands at the airports.

There is also concern about how the entry of organised retail will impact the small shops in the streets.

Here it needs to be underscored that even in many second world countries like Indonesia, Brazil, Venezuela, Colombia, Saudi Arabia, etc. where international hypermarkets contribute around or over 50 per cent of the trade, the balance half of the business yet takes place through the traditional corner stores, or the 'banias', 'hattis' (small grocers) concept of stores.

So, hypermarkets and malls do not mean the end of the small stores. In fact, many small stores continue to flourish. Customers do not visit hypermarkets at the drop of a hat. A visit to a large store has to be planned. For normal daily grocery purchases, consumers continue to visit the corner shop.

With the arrival of modern retailing and hypermarkets, the smaller neighbourhood stores invariably spruce up in terms of layout, presentation, merchandising and customer service. The entire trade becomes more customer conscious.

I have worked in many of these countries and have studied these trade dynamics and evolved distribution systems around these paradigms. In Brazil, Colombia, Venezuela, Ecuador, etc., small shops do roaring business despite the presence of global brands of hypermarkets like Carrefour and Walmart. In the Middle East countries like the UAE, Saudi Arabia, Oman, etc., hypermarkets contribute around 65 to 70 per cent of sales, the balance 30 per cent of sales are yet generated by small shops. The Abu Dhabi Municipality has also introduced a plan for improving the presentation, merchandising and layouts of small grocery shops.

The Modern Trade and small retail shops co-exist harmoniously in Brazil to serve the vast population, across the country. A case study entitled, 'Brazil: Coexistence of Modern Trade with Wholesalers and Small Retail shops: Garments business', is presented in the next section.

The new supermarket operators in India should have plans to absorb some of the smaller vendors who could be displaced, so that the latter would also be ensured of continued livelihoods.

So, we should welcome global brands to India and let the consumers spend in India itself. Otherwise, Indians who travel abroad to London, New York, Singapore, Hong Kong or Dubai will buy their Rolexes, Guccis, Versaces or Armanis abroad.

Some years ago when I lived in Brazil, and I returned to India on my annual leave, I would be buying my requirements from London airport. I used to be upset that I am expending foreign exchange at foreign airports, simply because I was not sure whether the Indian airports would have the brands that I needed.

The story was diametrically opposite when I returned to Sao Paulo after my annual leave. Sao Paulo has a massive supermarket, as a duty free shop. Brazilians and tourists travelling to Sao Paulo did not need to buy anything abroad. The duty free supermarket at the Sao Paulo airport after arrivals has everything you needed to buy.

MY EXPERIENCES IN MODERN RETAIL

Foreign Direct Investment (FDI) in Retail:

Permitting Foreign Direct Investment in multi-branded Retail will encourage large retailers like Metro, Tesco, Carrefour, etc. to view India favourably as an investment destination. The entry of these international players will usher a new paradigm in retailing.

FDI in retail will facilitate: expansions of the product range for the Indian consumer, professional management, latest inventory management techniques, IT systems, management development and training.

Impact of Rising Costs of Retail:

A rise in costs of real estate is a pure function of the demand and supply equation. So, as retailers seek incremental space for their concepts and malls, prices of land and rentals will see escalation. This is natural and to be expected, as everywhere in the world.

Retailers will expand their operations beyond the existing city limits and borders. A large hypermarket would need 1,00,000 to 2,00,000 square feet for a good quality outlet. It would be smart to position such large outlets outside the cities, where the land and rentals are cheaper. These hypermarket concepts come with restaurants, etc., and would become weekend shopping outlets.

A concept like Ikea, would need 2,00,000 to 5,00,000 square feet for a good quality outlet in Delhi or Mumbai. It would be smart to position such outlets, just outside the cities, where the land and the rentals would be cheaper. Ikea outlets come with restaurants, etc., and would be a shopping outlet for the customers over a weekend.

Cities also grow and expand. Perhaps in a few decades the space considered outside the city today, would be the city Centre. Dazzling shopping facilities, surrounded by hotels, can also boost tourism. One has to play long in business in general, and in retailing in particular.

The real estate and mall developers will also gain from appreciation in their assets' prices. These builders and investors are investing their moneys in buildings and retail concepts on the basis of their faith in the consumers and the future.

So, if they become rich, well they deserve to.

MY EXPERIENCES IN MODERN RETAIL

CASE STUDY:
BRAZIL: COEXISTENCE OF MODERN TRADE WITH WHOLESALERS AND SMALL RETAIL SHOPS: GARMENTS BUSINESS

Modern Trade retail shops can and do coexist harmoniously with small shops, as this case study of Brazil, concerning ready-made garments, clearly shows.

Background Brazil's potential:

Brazil is a vast market with a population of 206 million people, whose living standard has been improving. About 86 per cent of the population lives in urban areas. The per capita GDP of the country is USD 11,900 and the GDP of the country is USD 2.32 trillion. The country has the fifth largest area in the world, divided into 26 states, and is witnessing all-round development. Brazil's formal market for apparel is estimated to be around USD 40 billion.

Due to the policies of income re-distribution followed by successive governments, the lot of the economically weaker sections, particularly in the Northeast e.g. Fortaleza, Manaus, Belem, etc., has been improving sharply. They have more purchasing power, than they had two decades ago.

The rich and upper class population has grown from 26.4 million in 2005 to 42.2 million in 2010 with an increase of about 60 per cent; whereas the population of middle class grew from 62.7 million in 2005 to 101.7 million in 2010 with an increase of around 62 per cent. However, the lower income population declined from 93 million in 2005 to 48 million in 2010, i.e. a decline of 48 per cent.

Brazilians are highly figure, look and fashion conscious. The women particularly, spend money on looking good and dressing elegantly; they are sophisticated and well informed. Brands like Diane von Furstenberg, Missoni, Chanel, Gucci, Louis Vuitton and Burberry have made large investments in opening stores in major towns principally in Sao Paulo, but also in the capital Brasilia, a fast emerging market for luxury goods. Gucci's Sao Paulo boutique is one of the brand's top performing stores globally.

Brazilian shopping culture:

Brazilians love shopping. They shop for clothes, footwear, food, furniture, household products, etc. Most Brazilians shop at High Streets, malls and 'fieras' (Sunday bazaars, i.e. 'domingo fiera').

Some of the large Modern Retail stores and Hypermarkets of ready-made garments, operating in Brazil are:

1) Renner–Retail chain:

Renner is the second largest retailer in Brazil with 191 retail outlets and plans to reach 533 outlets by 2021. It has a turnover of around USD 2 billion. The Company started as a textile unit in 1912, pioneered by Mr. Anthony Renner. The first retail store was inaugurated in 1922. Today, it is a public company, traded on the stock exchange.

The company invests heavily in research and design. It also offers financial services to its customers and currently there are 19 million Renner cardholders. They focus sharply on quality and price.

MY EXPERIENCES IN MODERN RETAIL

The highlights are:

a) They have 171 stores and operate in the mall framework; hence, 93 per cent of their outlets are in malls.

b) Their outlets range in size from 2,000 to 3,000 square metre.

c) They also own a 33 retail store chain 'Camicado' specialising in Home. These Home outlets are about 500 square metres each.

d) They have 15 private labels, segmented by lifestyle. They also have labels for footwear and cosmetics.

2) Riacheulo –retail chain:

This chain of retail outlets comprises of 180 outlets. This department store company commenced operations in 1947 and has a large production and distribution base in Natal state. It is a well-managed, professional Group.

Riacheulo is the No.3 retailer in Brazil, after C&A and Renner. The Company employs about 40,000 people and has a turnover of USD 1.3 billion. The company produces about three million pieces annually.

3) Marisa retail chain:

Marisa is another large retailing firm in Brazil. They have the largest number of retail outlets in Brazil at about 350. Their outlets are located in Malls and also in High Streets e.g. Paulista Avenue, the main financial artery of the country. Marisa specialises in women's clothing and accessories, though they also do men's and kids' clothing and accessories.

The prices of their products are mid-scale and the brand is well positioned amongst middle class consumers. Marisa has a turnover of USD 1.3 billion and employs 14,000 people.

4) Hypermarket - Pao de Acucar:

Pao de Acucar Group has about 1,800 stores in the country, through different formats and banners. Pao de Acucar operates about 169 supermarkets and its sister-concern 'Extra' operates 135 hypermarkets and 200 supermarkets. They also have 900 electronics stores across the country. It is the largest retailer in Brazil, followed by Carrefour.

a) They sell basics, fashion and sports lines, but in the middle price segments.

b) It is owned by the Casino Group in France. Although the entire Group in managed singly as far as the finances are concerned, the two retail entities i.e. Pau de Acucar and Extra, are managed as independent profit centers.

5) Hypermarket: Walmart:

Walmart is another large retailer in Brazil, after Pao de Acucar and Carrefour. They bought a popular and strong local group of supermarkets, called 'Bompreco' (Good price), which has strengthened their position in Northeastern Brazil, in the Bahia and Pernambuco states.

MY EXPERIENCES IN MODERN RETAIL

6) Hypermarket - Carrefour:

Carrefour commenced operations in Brazil in 1975 and is a major player in Brazil, across all states. It has 150 hypermarkets and 38 supermarkets, along with 350 discount and convenience stores.

Malls:

Shopping malls are multiplying across Brazil, even in medium sized towns like Salvador, Porto Alegre, Recife, Fortaleza, etc. They are major avenues for shopping for clothes, but are also popular eating-places.

Sao Paulo has over 50 shopping Malls. The most popular and important ones are:

1) J.K. Iguatemi Mall: This is relatively a new Mall, for top-end luxury brands

2) Morumbi mall: An upper middle class mall, with many local fashion brands.

3) Iguatemi Mall: An upper middle class mall, with many local fashion brands.

4) Shopping Centre Norte: A very popular, middle class mall.

5) Shopping Eldorado: Popular middle class mall, located in a premium locality, Jardins.

6) Shopping Paulista Mall: Functional, popular mall, located in the main Paulista Avenue, mainly local brands.

High Streets:

In addition to the retail groups, hypermarkets and malls selling ready-made garments, Brazil has flourishing High Street markets.

Brazilians love shopping in the High Streets. Every city/town has designated area/streets renowned for some brands. The most fashionable street in the country, 'Rua Oscar Freire', in Sao Paulo has all the top fashionable brands from the world and the country. 'Oscar Freire' is renowned as one of the top eight fashionable streets in the world.

Shops located on Rua Oscar Freire and surrounding crossing streets on Rua Bela Cintra and Rua Haddock Lobo include Louis Vuitton, Armani, Dior, Montblanc, Cartier, MaxMara, Ermenegildo Zegna, Versace, Diesel, Cavalli, Bulgari, Salvatore Ferragamo, Gant, Lacoste, Timberland, Tommy Hilfiger, Nike, Adidas and Benetton.

The top Brazilian fashion brands like Alexandre Herchcovitch, Animale, Forum, Ellus, Sergio K, Havaianas, Cavalera, Le Lis Blanc, Canal, Triton, high end jewelry stores e.g. H Stern are also located on this street.

Other large towns in Brazil like Rio, Belo Horizonte, Porto Alegre and Recife have similar star outlet streets, though not in the same class as Oscar Freire.

The habit of shopping in the High Streets is the reason that many top fashion brands in the country have some stores located in them.

MY EXPERIENCES IN MODERN RETAIL

'Feiras':

'Fieras' are informal markets organised in important streets and squares, on holidays or Sundays. There are different types of 'fieras' selling fruits, vegetables, fish, handicrafts, paintings, foods and even clothes.

Brazilian Brands:

Brazilian home-grown brands are very popular in the country. Brazilian brands like Brooksfield, Siberian, Via Veneto, Harry's, Brooksfield Donna, Kids, have stores in Malls and High Streets across the country. Kids' brands like Joana Joao have also built franchise over the years.

Brazil's local luxury brand market is also booming. A case is Osklen sportswear, founded by an orthopaedic physician Oskar Metsavaht, having a turnover of around USD 200 million and selling T-shirts for USD 400 and tennis shoes for USD 200 in its 63 stores. Many Brazilians gravitate towards local fashion brands rather than global ones.

It is significant, that in Rua Oscar Freire, the most fashionable street in Latin America, there are as many Brazilian fashion brand outlets, as there are global ones.

Many local brands are manufactured in Brazil itself, though there is some importation from China, Peru, Bangladesh, India, etc.

Most of the local brands have 20 to about 70 outlets and may not form a sizeable opportunity in the initial stages.

It needs to be underscored that local brands tend to be highly fashionable and are often associated with local celebrities, like XuXa, a TV celebrity.

Wholesale markets for garments:

There are two important wholesale markets for garments in Sao Paulo. The first is in Jose Paulino and the second is in a neighbourhood called Braca.

The key observations are:

1) There are about 1,500 to 2,000 outlets in Jose Paulino and about 3,500 to 4,000 outlets in the Braca neighbourhood.

2) These outlets sell mainly women's apparel and some children's apparel. Men's clothing sells mainly in the Braca. The outlets are large, some about 5,000 square feet.

3) Even though these are wholesale outlets, the outlets are well planned and laid-out; they are also elegantly merchandised in most cases as in retail outlets.

4) The apparel sold in these markets is principally made in Brazil, China, Korea, Bangladesh, Peru and India.

5) The customers of these shops are varied. Small shopkeepers from Sao Paulo and other towns in the country visit these markets to buy stocks to sell locally. There are regular bus services from upcountry towns, which bring groups of customers to these markets in the mornings and then ferry them back in the evening.

6) Many upper class Paulista residents also visit the wholesale markets, to buy single pieces, for which they do pay a higher price, but even then, the prices are lower than the malls or High Streets.

7) These markets also have wholesale and retail shoes shops and outlets of other accessories required for doing up a retail apparel outlet e.g. mannequins, hangars, fittings, etc.

8) Key wholesalers, who import products, play a major role in these markets.

Conclusion:

It is clear from this case study that in a developing country malls, hypermarkets, large Retail Groups and the wholesale and small retail shops can all co-exist to serve the customer and grow the market. There are distinct needs of customers, which varying retail formats fulfil.

7
HARVESTING INDIA'S RURAL RETAIL POTENTIAL

Roshan a farmer in village Berni, used to travel 50 kilometres to Etah, Uttar Pradesh (U.P.) state to buy his requirements of cooking oil, soaps, tea, batteries, clothes and bulbs, for his family. Today, these products are available freely in his village. Roshan's wife Verrandevi, makes these purchases herself, on a weekly basis. She watches television every evening and is aware of various brands and the promises they make. She is also a great fan of the Indian cricket team.

Bittulal, a grocer in Sarwat village, near Muzaffarnagar (in U.P.) observes, "A decade ago I stocked about 300 items in my shop. Today, the consumer has become more demanding. He asks for many products by name. If I cannot give him 'Maxfresh' toothpaste, he scampers to next shop. So, now, I have to stock about 1,000 items."

The life styles and purchasing patterns of rural consumers are undergoing a significant metamorphosis. Widespread availability of consumer products in the small towns and villages, is changing the lives of rural consumers. Exposure to electronic media like TV and radio has made the rural consumer more aware, conscious and discriminating. Mobile phones and Internet have also brought them closer to consumer products.

With the gradual expansion of the Modern Retail formats in the cities and towns of India, many retailers have started eyeballing the over 640,000 villages for launching the self-service concepts of shopping. The entry of Modern Retail formats in the rural areas will also revolutionise shopping habits in the villages and create massive employment.

Importance of rural markets:

Indian rural consumers are undergoing a major metamorphosis is their buying habits and consumption patterns due to improvements in living conditions.

Rural India now contributes to half of the national market for many FMCG categories of products.

The next few decades could see massive increases in the spending powers of those who live in villages today. Villages will not be villages, any more, in the next few decades, in terms of consumption habits. They will commence merging into small town-urban buying habits. Rural areas will however, stay, in India for a long time to come. The urban population of India is expected to grow to about 34 per cent, by 2020. Thus, even in 2020, 66 per cent of India will yet live in the countryside.

Note again: According to MART, a New Delhi based research organisation, rural India buys 46 per cent of soft drinks, 49 per cent of motorcycles and 59 per cent of cigarettes, sold in India. Moreover, 11 per cent of rural women use lipstick.

The spending power of rural landowners and rural labour will augment very sharply. The population of India is expected to escalate from 1.21 billion in 2011 to almost 1.53 billion by 2030. India will be the highest populated country in the world, with China stabilising at 1.46 billion by 2030.

Now, these 1.53 billion people need to eat food, thrice a day. However, the landmass of India is fixed. It is not elastic. So, more productive agricultural technologies will be required to boost food production. Thus, another Green Revolution is in the offing. This will enrich the rural areas.

Consider: During the period 1980-81 to 2014-15, i.e. in 35 years, food grains production in India augmented from about 130 million tonnes to about 252 million tonnes. The miraculous phenomenon is that during the same period, the area under agricultural crops remained steady at around 125-150 million hectares. In the next 30 years, to feed another 300 million Indians, as also to feed another 250 million who will rise above the poverty line, India will have to augment agricultural production by about 70 to 100 per cent. This may sound intimidating, but is possible.

Expect food prices also to increase due to greater demand. Farmers and agricultural labour may be the central beneficiaries, due to the higher demand and prices of food.

In the next three decades, the villages of India will receive a lot of developmental expenditure, which will enrich rural dwellers. Corporations and retailers will increasingly be dedicating incremental time, manpower and resources to selling in the villages. The transformation from an urban to rural focus will be a key challenge facing Indian businessmen and retailers.

The tapping of the rural market will be very onerous for Indian retailers. Some companies have made dedicated efforts to set up distribution apparatuses in the rural areas. However, most manufacturers in India have relied on the robust wholesale network in semi-urban markets to feed the villages and interiors. Most companies have shied away from setting up distribution networks in the villages due to the massive commitments of management and money that is entailed.

Companies like Reliance, ITC, Godrej, Airtel, etc., have made commendable endeavours to take some new retail and retail service models to the villages. These efforts need to be accelerated.

Characteristics of rural consumers:

Retailers, who wish to set-up self-service format stores in the villages, need to understand the characteristics and behavioural patterns of these rural consumers. Some of the key characteristics of the emerging rural consumers are:

1)   Quality of life:

Increased incomes and improved awareness levels have made the villager seek a better quality of life. The rural consumer now demands a wider range of consumer durables and non-durables. Rural housewives crave for products like stoves and pressure cookers, which make cooking for the family easier and faster. The rural housewife also desires to choose her clothes from a wider variety of fabrics and designs.

2)   Brand-consciousness:

Rural consumers are now more knowledgeable about the availability of the different brands of a product. Two decades ago, a rural consumer would go to a shop and merely ask for a tablet of soap. He would use the same tablet for bathing as well as for washing his clothes. Today, the same villager asks for a bathing soap by its brand name. He also buys toothpaste and asks for it by brand name.

3) Willingness to innovate:

The rural consumer is no longer suspicious of new urban products. He is willing to innovate and experiment with new products. This makes it easier for manufacturers to get higher trial rates, when new products are launched in the villages. Mobile phones have taken the rural areas by storm. A mobile phone is no longer a status symbol in the villages. It is already perceived as 'must-have' necessity.

4) Fashion-consciousness:

The villager is becoming more conscious of how he or she looks and grooms. Sales of textiles are on the increase. Villagers are also buying garments like shirts, trousers, shorts and frocks for children. In a village called Achrol, about 45 kilometres from Jaipur, (Rajasthan) shops sell ready-to-wear garments. The market for cosmetics is growing rapidly in the rural market.

5) Role of women:

The influx of consumer products in the villages has highlighted the role of the rural housewife. She has now become a key influencer and decision maker in all buying decisions. A decade ago, consumer products were not easily available in the village. The farmer travelled 50 to 100 kilometres alone, unaccompanied by his wife, to a 'mandi' or feeder market to purchase household necessities. The farmer thus made the entire key buying decisions regarding the product or the brand to be purchased.

MY EXPERIENCES IN MODERN RETAIL

Today the rural housewife increasingly makes up her on mind about what she will buy for her family. The literacy rate among women in urban areas and the villages are improving steadily.

Potential for organised retail:

With augmented awareness levels, higher income levels and rising aspirations, the rural consumer is also a target for organised retail. The rural farmer or his wife would also relish a shopping experience that offers more options, variety and some minimal pleasure.

However, an entry into rural markets will have to be determined by the following variables:

1) Population strata - Feeder markets:

Organised retail should focus on markets, which are traditionally a fulcrum for wholesalers to supply products to the retailers in smaller villages. A small feeder market could have a population of around 50,000, but the larger feeder markets, could have a population of as high as 500,000. Feeder markets allure customers from 100 to 250 surrounding villages. They would contribute to the sustainability of a Modern Retail store.

2) Per capita incomes:

A pioneering organised Modern Retail outlet would do well to focus on states with higher per capita farm incomes, to improve chances of success. Rural retail concepts will do well in states like Punjab, Haryana, Maharashtra and Gujarat. Higher rural per capita incomes will enable rapid acceptance of organised retail in the rural markets.

3) Type of Products:

The products which will enjoy high acceptability in the rural areas are:

a) Agricultural inputs like, seeds, fertilisers, pesticides, etc.,
b) Agricultural machinery and implements required for farming,
c) Transport equipment like tractors, two-wheelers, etc.

The product range will vary depending on the local demand. A very successful chain of supermarkets in Cote d'Ivoire, sells premium perfumes and designer apparel in the urban areas in the capital Abidjan. However, in the upcountry rural markets of Bouake it even sells live cocks, hens and goats!

The sales of lifestyle products like garments, footwear etc., will also spiral in the villages, with increased prosperity. Retailers, marketing economically priced lifestyle products will find a growing market in the villages.

Modern retailers will have to undergo a serious mind-set metamorphosis, to harvest rural markets. Marketing and selling to rural consumers is vastly different from marketing to urban consumers. Advertising and promotions, deployed in the urban areas, do not always deliver in villages.

MY EXPERIENCES IN MODERN RETAIL

Guidelines to entry:

In tapping the rural markets, retailers need to focus on long-term goals. Some guidelines are provided below:

1) Invest for the long term:

In some urban markets, high real estate prices and rentals have deterred retailers. For instance, there were no large supermarkets or hypermarkets, in Mumbai, all the way from Dadar to Andheri, despite the existence of a vibrant market for quite some time. In the rural markets also, many retail outlets may not yield quick returns. Retailers should yet pursue such ventures and perceive them as seeding operations. Retailers in the villages should be mentally prepared to wait for about three to four years to make profits.

2) Carry local community:

Urban retail growth has also been hampered by protests from neighbourhood grocers, hawkers, etc. Rural retailers should ensure that they blend harmoniously with the rural ethos and environment, to avoid operating environment issues. The key opinion leaders in the villages like the headman or 'sarpanch' or the schoolteacher should be briefed in advance.

3) Keep the outlets 'spacy':

To ensure that the rural consumer enjoys his shopping, there should be free space to move around the aisles in the outlet. Many retail outlets in the urban areas are severely hampered in aisle space, due to size constraints. A renowned and respected

Indian industrialist had once opined, "Calculate the space that you need for your business today. Then multiply it by three. Then buy it today!" This is sound advice for any business, including retail. If the business model is right, it is bound to grow and it may not be possible to get adjoining, incremental space later.

4)   Train your talent:

Many retailers tend to neglect training their staff adequately. Now training is required in manifold areas. Floor staff needs to be trained in selling, managing customers, handling complaints, computerised billings, etc. However, they also need to be taught the importance of good grooming, politeness, etc. In retail outlets we sell products, but the store too, is a product!

5)   Harvest rigorously, before expanding:

Retailers aiming to conquer the villages could do well to harvest a state or geographical zone rigorously, rather than spread across the country rapidly. Depth of coverage in a state/zone should supersede national width. Consumers are the same across the globe, but they have their nuances. These nuances need to be studied and appropriate business models gradually perfected.

Infrastructural impediments:

There are many infrastructural impediments to the entry of Modern Retail in the villages.

MY EXPERIENCES IN MODERN RETAIL

1)   Weak road networks:

Many remote villages are connected by mud roads or bullock cart paths to feeder markets. Lack of roads to connect villages to wholesale markets, results in convoluted supply lines and prices.

2)   Power supply:

Many villages across the country do not have electrical connections. Those areas that do have electricity, suffer numerous power cuts. Even the capital of the county New Delhi is not spared from these power cuts. How do you sell electric irons or televisions, in villages, which are yet to see an electric bulb?

3)   Water shortages:

Many Indian villages lack adequate access to potable and clean drinking water. These villages rely on wells or pumps. When there is a drought, these villages, have to scrounge for miles for a bucket of drinking water.

Statistics show that around 90 per cent of Indians have access to water. However, I have personally travelled to countless villages, which yet have wells or hand pumps only. In summer, these sources of water can run dry. How does one sell water heaters, in villages, which do not have water at all?

4) Warehousing and logistics bottlenecks:

The availability of warehouses is vital for effective logistics and retailing. Good quality warehousing facilities may not be easily available in the rural hinterland. Thus retailers who embark on the rural retail odyssey may have to build warehouses. This will increase entry costs. However, involving local third parties can minimise these costs.

5) Availability of suitable manpower:

The rural hinterland may not have adequate and appropriate manpower. Retailing requires educated, quality staff, i.e. salesmen, customer-service staff, service providers, IT personnel, etc. They may be difficult to find in the rural areas. So, companies will have to lure staff from the cities and smaller towns to work in the rural areas. These staff members will have to be motivated to accept the slower lifestyle in the villages.

One last point – Execution:

Sound and seamless execution is the soul of any business success. It is not very difficult to conceptualise new business models and paradigms. However, success depends on brilliant execution. Therefore, a seamless entry of retailers in the villages will require able managers, who have the grit and tenacity to rough it out in new markets and actually build and run modern stores in tough conditions.

MY EXPERIENCES IN MODERN RETAIL

Summary – Potential vs. appropriate models:

To summarise, Indian villages offer immense potential for the self-service format of Modern Retail stores. However, retailers will have to evolve new, simpler business models to serve the rural consumer. Specific entries into rural markets by retailers have to be discerning and minutely thought through in a business plan encompassing regions, localities, product range and back office processes.

Savitri, who lives in a shanty and works in homes in Mumbai, epitomises the dream of the New India of 2040. She has a home and plot of land in Paud, a small village in the heart of the Mulshi valley in Maharashtra. About 4,000 people live in the village, which has 300 odd shops.

As the prices of agricultural produce rise, Savitri is constantly mulling whether to return home, work on her own land and start a shop there. "I already have a mobile phone," she tells me. She is educating her son. "In my village only two families have a computer. I am saving money to buy a computer for my son. Then he will be able to work from my home in the village. And, I can return to Paud," Savitri tells me. She is beaming at the prospect of returning to her family village sometime soon.

8
WANTED BY RETAIL INDIA: 'THE ENTREPRENEURIAL MANAGER'

Retail India will need a new breed of entrepreneurial managers to jump-start new product concepts and fight tough competition, in the new retail millennium. The advent of modern retailing over the next two decades, will kindle serious discontinuities in the shopping patterns and behaviour of consumers. Competition will also be swifter and tougher, necessitating business leaders with strong entrepreneurial drives.

These leaders should be positioned at apex levels, to ensure percolation of dynamism throughout the organisation. They must drive change and profits. They have to innovate with new retail offerings.

The Indian Retail environment, in the next two decades, will be characterised by:

1) Rapid urban expansion: India needs hypermarkets, of 1,00,000 square feet and above in the coming future.

2) Intense competition from local and foreign entrants: Carrefour, Walmart, Lulu, etc., will enter India. Local operators should welcome competition. It sharpens performance.

3) Growth of online shopping and e-commerce: Amazon and Flipkart are gradually but definitely, revolutionising shopping

habits in India. Millions of products are available to Indian shoppers with a click. Products are delivered to their homes on Cash on Delivery basis.

4) Expansion in the interior and rural areas: Over 850 million people reside in the villages of India. Retailers should start tapping the hinterlands, with new low priced concept and formats.

5) Increasingly discriminating, price sensitive and disloyal consumers: With augmented offerings, consumers could be as fickle in brand loyalties. They will have to be wooed continuously.

6) Surcharged operating environment: Some parties and local retailers may resist organised and Modern Retail advances. However, progress will continue.

Despite tremendous strides, there are vital challenges confronting Indian retail. Our malls can be better planned. The roads circumscribing the malls are broken and not very user friendly. Some malls and outlets have cracked tiles on the floors. Many outlets and even malls, have inadequately trained and poorly dressed staff. Some staff members cannot speak English. We need to focus on improving toilets, sanitation and natural light. Customer service also needs to sharpen. If your shirt size is not available, nobody gets it for you next day. You are informed, "It is not there." Sometimes, the salesman tells you with a wink, "Try our clothes, before buying. Our sizes are often incorrect!"

Many cashiers at the tills, cannot bill a sales promotion. Fruits and vegetables could be cleaned or displayed attractively. The delivery boy should close the door of the car gently. Many retailers are struggling to manage the environment.

Yet, India abounds in retail opportunities, like no other nation. The 1.3 billion consumers in the urban and rural markets, if segmented by income, age, sex and class of town offer a plethora of opportunities to smart retailers. The opportunities abound in every product category from brooms to books, washbasins to watches, sweets to suits, apples to automobiles and from eggs to eggplants. The monolithic Indian markets out there, waiting for smart retailers. India is a massive market of many segments. Retailers just have to segment it adroitly.

So, we need strong, entrepreneurial managers to propel Retail India, to global standards.

Characteristics of Entrepreneurial Retail Managers: New Breed, New Creed!

These entrepreneurial managers would combine visionary skills with high action orientation, possess strong leadership skills and be at mid-career levels. Their superiors may have classified them as 'mavericks' in the past, but they would be deliverers. They would be professional, but subdued on organisational loyalty depending on how they grow and how well they are treated. They would be characterised as:

1) Having sound knowledge of the market:

They would have profound knowledge of consumers, trading patterns and wholesale markets. Indian retailing has to be highly supply chain oriented. Rigorous knowledge of trading patterns and middlemen behaviour is crucial to becoming a successful retailer.

MY EXPERIENCES IN MODERN RETAIL

Retail will rapidly permeate to Class B towns e.g. Pune, Chandigarh, etc. and Class C towns e.g. Kolhapur, Jalandhar, etc. too. Retail will also percolate down to rural India, with formats to sell agricultural inputs and farm implements. Therefore, the new retailers should have their ears close to the villages.

2) Defeat-busters:

These managers are principally self-driven, set ambitious personal and corporate goals. They take strong risks to progress the business and their own careers. They would be managers, who do not give up, ever. They defy defeat. Retail is fiercely competitive. Walmart, Carrefour, Tesco, etc., compete agonisingly, for every cent. We need tough negotiators to head retail businesses.

Mr. Micky Jagtiani, Chairman of the Landmark Group, which owns the popular retail brands Shoe Mart, Baby Shop, Home Centre, etc., commenced his career driving a cab in London. Nevertheless, he believed in his dream and destiny. Today, he is one of the largest retailers in the Middle East, with successful concepts in apparel, homes, etc. He is a retail pioneer.

3) Visionaries:

Certainly the entrepreneurial managers would be visionaries who would be capable of strong action. They operate beyond traditional boundaries and spot new opportunities, markets and successes. They buffer beliefs with courageous action. Charting new paths involves negotiations with established conventions, rules, manuals and power structures.

A recent addition to Dubai's electronics market is the Sharaf DG (Digital Galleria) concept, led by the flagship 1,00,000 square feet electronic store, stocking everything in the category. Their 20 plus outlets are redefining the paradigms of the electronics market in the Middle East. The Sharaf DG brand is rated amongst the Top 10 Brands in the UAE. The Store also has a policy of promoting from within and candidates, who joined as salesmen, have grown into store managers.

The management has also started an online store for customers in view of the competition form online retailers.

4) Mid-career professionals:

Typically, these entrepreneurial managers would be mid-career professionals, with 15 to 20 years' experience. A certain minimum personal maturity is a prerequisite to taking risks with a company's agenda and money. These professionals would have a track record of overcoming adversities i.e. delivering in tough markets, defeating established competitors and building robust teams. They would be men who have turned defeats into successes.

5) 'Mavericks':

These entrepreneurial retail managers may not fit in conventional descriptions. They could have been classified as 'cranks', 'unconventional 'and 'bizarre' at a selection. However, if we are searching for leaders, who redraw maps, we will need entrepreneurs who challenge normal classifications. They would typically command fierce loyalty from their teams.

MY EXPERIENCES IN MODERN RETAIL

The legendary Sam Walton was, perhaps termed a 'maverick', when he commenced his entrepreneurial voyage. He went around meeting supermarkets operators, making copious notes, in fat notebook, to the amazement of the people he was interviewing. He was learning retailing at the ground level.

'Haldiram', was the name of a sweetmeat shop some years ago. Today it is a major FMCG brand in sweets and packaged savouries. It is a preferred retail brand not merely in Kolkata or Delhi, but in many parts of the world. The 'Haldiram' Retail concept could be scalable for other cities and smaller towns. It would also be successful in foreign markets with large Indian populations like USA, UK, etc.

6) 'Mercenary breed':

These entrepreneurial managers may not be outstandingly loyal to the organisations they work for, in terms of long-term careers. However, they would be ruthlessly professional in their dealings e.g. confidentiality, ethics, etc. They would also be a bit mercenary and seek bonuses, profit sharing and stock options from their employers. Organisations do not guarantee life-long employment, anymore. So, there is an emerging breed of managers, whose professional careers are from contract to contract. Driven by professional egos, they build strong teams.

How Do We Find Entrepreneurial Managers?

Retail businesses may unearth such entrepreneurial managers, by tracking men who have swivelled failed markets and brands into successes. Such entrepreneurial managers can also be recognised, by trailing major market and brand successes.

1) Within the retail business:

Most companies would have 10 to 15 per cent of its managers in this entrepreneurial category. The real skill will be in finding these future leaders. We could also identify managers who are entrepreneurial, but have got passed by, due to a sporadic mishap or plain oversight. These are the change agents we are hunting for. Examine the career paths of managers who may have been on the 'High Potential' bandwagon, but then disembarked due to some mishap. They may have tucked away their troubles and are raring to go again.

Within retail groups, there are managers, who have rejuvenated dull stores, revitalised frail retail concepts, and sharpened sloppy teams into great performers. They have turned failures into successes through vision, drive, systems and teams. Most strong leaders are individualists, not necessarily team players. It is an embattled Prime Minister Winston Churchill or a rugged General George Patton that we seek.

2) Poaching:

Retail India will also need to poach aggressively from other retail companies all over the world. We can study successful retail groups, concepts; probe the leaders who are responsible for these accomplishments and lure them by offering them challenges and opportunities.

3) Train Young Managers:

Retail India should inculcate entrepreneurial values among younger managers, through training programs, to ensure percolation of a restless, searching spirit among potential leaders. Their role models have to be Bill Gates, Sam Walton and David Sainsbury.

How Do We Reward Entrepreneurial Managers?

1)   Give them space:

Strong and able retail leaders need space and freedom, to build teams and deliver results. Their jobs are frequently unstructured; they have to introduce new systems and processes. If anyone breathes down their neck, they rebel. Many a CEO moans in private, "I hate being second-guessed." Others lament, "I have committed a profit figure to the company. I will hand them a cheque on 1 January, but they must leave me alone to deliver." Another bemoans, "They tie my hands and feet, and then they want me to win the Olympics!"

Leaders need to be left alone sometimes, to deliver.

2)   Pay more than market:

These entrepreneurial managers have to be paid competitively. Change agents are risk-intoxicated. They take personal career perils with the ambitious goals they set for themselves and their companies. They also jeopardise their reputations. Failure is expensive for them in terms of credibility and career. Correspondingly, success should ensure gorgeous rewards for them to be motivated. Since career-spans in companies could get abbreviated in the future, monetary rewards could make entrepreneurial managers raise the bar after each lap.

3) Immediate Returns:

These managers prefer high immediate rewards, i.e. cash bonuses and stock options as compared to retirement benefits. These entrepreneurial managers could be receiving cash bonuses up to 100 per cent or more of their annual salaries, for turning around a business.

How to Retain and 'Re-energise' Entrepreneurial Managers?

1) Back to the drawing board:

Retail companies should review whether operating environments and reward systems foster the entrepreneurial manager. Excessive regimentation should not curb creativity, which is a staple spur in an entrepreneur.

2) Rewarding and retaining them:

High monetary rewards and faster rises to tougher jobs, are the keys to rewarding and retaining this group of emerging entrepreneurial managers.

3) Financial trophies:

For such entrepreneurial managers, the best reward is an even tougher job! However, unless the retail group is growing rapidly, it may not be possible to keep adding to the responsibilities of such managers. Then, financial trophies, i.e. bonuses and profit-sharing schemes, can motivate them. Smart retail organisations, will have profit sharing schemes for their CEOs.

Chairman's Challenge:

Retail businesses should refashion their operating environments to foster the emergence and flourishing of entrepreneurial managers. This would imply we respect and even reward failure in innovation if there were lessons to be imbibed, be more tolerant of unconventional conduct and be less regimented in assessment of potential. So, top management will have to be more judicious.

Finally, if a top deliverer does decide to bid adieu to the organisation, send him with the best farewell party money can buy. Send him with all his dues paid. Never send out these leaders with a sigh. Let them go out with a smile. They are your ambassadors to the world at large.

The challenge for retail India in the next two decades will be to evolve organisational structures and cultures to be market leaders and yet rejoice entrepreneurship and individual initiative at all levels.

That will be the key challenge for the retail Chairman.

9

IS INDIAN RETAIL FLOUNDERING?

"Let's just go to Ikea, to buy the wardrobe," suggested my friend Isabella, as we trudged through the streets of Kalbadevi road and Mohammed Ali road, avoiding a plethora of potholes. I did not know how to respond to her for Ikea has not yet started operations in India. Later, as we hunted for buckets, rugs and crockery in a dozen outlets in overcrowded streets, pushed by hawkers and petrified of speeding taxis, Isabella counselled me innocently, "Let's go to Carrefour!"

In the evening, as we sipped cool tender coconut water (*'nariyal-pani'*), at Chowpatty beach, I explained to Isabella, "Look in India, we do not have an Ikea or Carrefour. We are a land of around 12 million grocery retail outlets, servicing 1.3 billion Indians. You see, 97 per cent of Indians shop in small shops!" Isabella was flabbergasted. "Why?" she queried.

Now, Isabella lives in Brazil and was helping me to furnish my apartment in Mumbai. For her, visiting a hypermarket in Rio de Janeiro like Extra Hipermercados, Bompreco, Supermercados Condor, Hipermercado Big, Walmart or a Zona Sul supermarket, to buy her daily requirements of fresh baked breads, imported cheeses, olives, French Bordeaux wines, fruits and vegetables, was as simple as brushing her teeth every morning!

So, I explained patiently to Isabella, "There are rules about permitting multi-product retailers to operate in the country. Even single brand retailers like Nike are permitted to operate with a specific quantum of foreign investment. The entry of big-players like Ikea, could throw thousands of small carpenters out of business."

"However," she argued, "a global household products retailer like Ikea could revolutionise the quality of daily living in lower and middle income categories. You say that many carpenters would be unemployed. Nevertheless, thousands of carpenters are already troubled by the manufacturers of ready-made furniture. Observe: the half to full page advertisements in newspapers of ready-made wardrobes and sofa sets."

I pondered over her comments. True, the entry of retailers like Ikea, Pottery Barn, Crate & Barrel, could raise standards in the Indian market.

"Furthermore, if these modern retailers agree to source even 25 per cent of their requirements locally, it will enrich Indian carpenters and add to their competencies and skills by modernising and updating their skills! Ikea could even source their products for global markets from here, adding wealth to Indian carpenters," lectured Isabella to me.

1) Policies:

Isabella's comments made sense to me. Perhaps we need to unshackle the retail sector further. There are yet serious restrictions on the entry of foreign retailers. Foreign investment in retailing is yet limited. This could stunt the growth of the retail sector, preventing generation of jobs, reduction of prices and vendor development in the country.

Despite the retailing revolution in India, the sad fact is that 'organised' outlets, or the 'modern-trade', comprising of supermarkets, hypermarkets and department stores, contributes around five to six per cent of the Indian retail market. The rest of the business takes place, principally through small groceries and 'Mom-and-Pop' stores.

The sons of these 'Mom-and-Pop" stores do not want to work in these mingy shops, anymore. In the new India, the new generation, dreams of becoming computer engineers, entrepreneurs, movie stars, etc.

The children of many shopkeepers spend more time in computer or dance classes, than in their parents' shops learning how to make a three per cent profit margin on the sales of wheat flour.

Indian retailers are in a learning mode. They do not have the experience, technologies, systems and processes, to run large format retail outlets on a massive national scale. Again, some local Indian supermarket operators chase quick profits. However, to sustain large format hypermarkets, one needs deep pockets and a long vision.

It is time for India to review the restrictions on foreign investment by multi-brand retailers, which prevents global retailers from opening stores and providing Indian consumers with a refreshing shopping experience .

Opening the Indian market to global retailers has the potential to provide enormous opportunities for small Indian businesses, through local sourcing and imparting of new technologies.

The most bountiful advantages of the entry of multiproduct global retailers will be in the agricultural sector. There will be significant enhancements in supply chain and logistics, expansion of road and warehouse networks. This will help to modernise the supply chain network, which will reduce wastages, cut rotting of vegetables and fruits and diminish the role of middlemen. This will also benefit the farmer through higher returns.

Consider the fiasco of the bizarre increase in the prices of onions and garlic, some years ago, which sent shockwaves across the country. The prices of onions skyrocketed from Rs. 30 per kilogram to Rs. 90 per kilogram, in a few weeks' time. Garlic also became an absolute luxury at Rs. 400 per kilogram. Many poor and lower middleclass families, simply deleted garlic and onions from their cuisines.

The reasons given for this bizarre price spiral were unseasonal rains, increase in demand, etc. Yet, there could have been mismanagement of stocks. Small vendors and hawkers cannot fight trade cartels. Large hypermarkets will hold adequate inventories, move stocks rapidly and ensure balanced prices.

It is well known that about 30 to 40 per cent of vegetables and fruits rot in India, due to inadequate storage and warehousing conditions in the country. Modern supermarkets can contribute to reduce these wastages. This will augment the earnings of the farmers and also reduce prices in the market.

Sure, there can be caveats on the entry of multi-product retailers, e.g. to generate local employment and to source some part of the products locally. These retailers could also source products from India for their global operations. This would create more wealth and opportunities for Indian entrepreneurs.

For instance, if retailers like Carrefour were to invest in India, with the condition that they source about 25 to 50 per cent of the products locally, it would open many global doors for local manufacturers.

2) Retailer disconnect with the environment:

India is going through a much fractured time. The rich are affluent and are making it to Global Wealth Lists. The middle classes love buying branded apparel and new mobile telephones. The lower middle classes, peer out of the windows of their small cars or metro trains, hoping to buy a bigger car or move to a two-bedroom apartment.

However, India also has many poor people. About 22 per cent of Indians (i.e. 290 million) yet live below the poverty line of USD 2 i.e. about Rs. 100 per day. This segment of Indian population has yet to benefit from India's growth. This group of people observes with some disquiet, how others are improving their living standards.

Drive through Dharavi in Mumbai, Asia's biggest slum, any day of the week, to see how the urban poor live. India's seven to eight per cent GDP growth is yet to touch them. A million citizens of Mumbai, live in this slum in tattered shops, tanneries, dilapidated warehouses and workshops.

The impoverished villagers and slum dwellers of India, have to be integrated, into the development processes in the towns and the villages. Failure to do so will create serious disturbances and slow the development process.

MY EXPERIENCES IN MODERN RETAIL

3) Infrastructural support:

Many malls could do better with improved infrastructure around them, and within too. The roads leading to the mall are frequently clogged with traffic.

Welcome to Lower Parel. The shopping lure in central Mumbai that houses some of the top brands in this bustling metropolis. The malls here house prestigious brands like Zara, Marks & Spencer, etc. However, it could take you almost 15 minutes to park your car and then walk to the retail outlets. Some of the best malls in Gurugram, have dilapidated approach roads.

Malls across the country could improve their clustering. A food outlet should not be next to a shoe store. A fashion store should not be next to an electronics store.

Many shopping zones and malls ignore the basic principle of 'cohesive clusters', whereby products with affinities are bunched together. This makes it easier for a shopper to check the full range of products in all the outlets in the mall.

The displays of merchandise in outlets, also needs additional professional focus. Augmented attention to overall aesthetics, lighting, presentation of the products will attract more customers and boost sales. Toilets in many malls need improved maintenance.

4) Real estate prices, rentals:

Perhaps the pivotal reason for the tardy progress of the retail sector in India is the high real estate prices and rentals prevailing in most cities.

The prices of real estate, especially in crowded cities like Mumbai, render mall and retail operations vulnerable. Rental cost should ideally be around five to 10 per cent of aggregate sales. High rentals can take this cost element to 15 to 25 per cent of sales. If rentals are very high, the outlet will struggle to breakeven.

High real estate prices could deter most large format retailers from commencing operations in major cities like Mumbai, Kolkata, Chennai, Bangalore, etc. The problem is exacerbated by the fact that the large retail formats, need parking space for over 1,000 cars upwards, depending on the shopping concepts housed in the complex. Parking space also costs money and adds to the overheads.

Due to the high real estate prices, many retail operations are commenced at available spaces, rather than in optimum catchment locations.

Real estate prices have also slowed down the rapid growth and expansion of the retail sector. The speed, with which Indian retail was supposed to flourish, has not happened.

5) Sizes of outlets:

Due to the exorbitant real estate prices, many retail concepts, compromise on the size of the outlets. Some of the modern trade grocery outlets in the metro cities that sell groceries, vegetables and fruits, are too small. Sometimes, the aisles are barely four to six feet wide, making it difficult for even two trolleys to pass each other simultaneously. Frequently inventories of fast moving vegetables like onions, potatoes, and tomatoes are not replenished fast enough due to space shortages.

Many of these new grocery outlets have only two or three checkout counters. Thus, during the evening hours, you could spend 30 minutes to select your vegetables, and then expend another 15 to 20 minutes to pay the bill, waiting your turn at the checkout counters.

Self-service grocery stores should endeavour to 'add value' to fresh vegetables and fruits by buying in bulk, cleaning, grading and repacking the vegetables and fruits in saleable units or packages (i.e. 500 grams to 1 kilogram packs). Grocery supermarkets can offer immense value to the consumers by offering cleaned and cut vegetables and fruits.

Many retail concepts often have to compromise on non-commercial areas like staff recreation, canteens and toilet areas in view of the tight space and high real estate prices and rentals.

6) Development of Retail centres or townships:

A provident and far-sighted step for many retailers and local governments would be, to set up retail centres or townships, a few kilometres outside the main town or city, as independent entities. These retail centres, could house large plus small retail formats, with a series of food courts and restaurants, ringed by gardens, parks and recreational facilities.

These retail centres should have six to eight lane roads leading from the city centre, straight to the complex, including dedicated metro services.

A good example of this is Wrentham Village outlets, about 45 minutes from Boston. The complex houses some of the best global brands e.g.: Burberry, Calvin Klein, Hugo Boss, Kenneth

Cole, Saks Fifth Avenue, etc. The open-air mall has excellent outlets, gardens, food courts, storage spaces, plus ATMs, strollers, wheelchairs, convenient transport facilities, broad lanes, etc. It also has a range of restaurants and eateries i.e. Buckhead Grill, Green Mountain Coffee, Jump Asian Express, Main Street Deli, Mrs. Fields, etc.

It is a delight to spend an entire day wafting in and out of the stores and the food outlets, in bright sunshine, circumvented by well-manicured grass lawns and multi-coloured flowers.

India's second and third tier of towns, e.g. Pune, Chandigarh, Lucknow, Bhubaneswar, Kochi and Baroda, should review creating retail centres, at 30 to 40 kilometres, outside the town centres. It would be wise to create these shopping paradises for families to have a wonderful time over the weekends.

Cities and towns increasingly need to keep a 25 to 50-year perspective in all their master planning exercises. Firm plans can continue for every five years, but within an aggregate, overall developmental perspective of 25 years.

7) Development of staff:

The staff in retail outlets should receive intensive training and development. Product knowledge should be emphasised in all retail outlets. Floor staff needs to be trained, to remember the value of a simple 'smile'!

A retail outlet is a place of work. Hence long and untidy hairstyles should be discouraged. Staff members should be coached in greetings, courtesies and dealing with customers.

Salaries of staff, especially at the shop floor and back office levels, should be reviewed at regular intervals depending on their performance. When a retailer does not have an internal promotion plan, then the incentive to excel is dulled.

We need to offer careers, not merely livelihoods or jobs. This is not a mere social responsibility or duty. It can make the retail operation a grand success.

8) Aesthetics – Looking Good, Feeling Good factors:

Retailers will also benefit from more attention to aesthetics and presentation of outlets and malls. Shopping zones and malls should have a theme or proposition. Architectural beauty and differentiation can augment sales.

An outstanding example of a themed mall is the Ibn Battuta Mall, in Dubai. It is one of the world's largest themed shopping mall and is designed to felicitate the travels and journeys of the famous Arab explorer Ibn Battuta. The Mall has over 275 retailers, 50 restaurants and food outlets, and 21 cinema screens. The Mall has Chinese, Indian, Egyptian, Persian, Tunisian and Andalusian Courts, with regional architecture, profiles and themes. The Food Courts and restaurants in these zones, serve cuisines from these countries/regions. It is a pleasure to visit the Mall, for it is a walk down the embellished lanes of history of many regions and countries.

The profit motive has a pivotal place in retail viability. However, customer service and customer joy need to become key drivers, for the profit goals to be met.

In the ultimate analysis, retailing is rigorous work.

10

RETAIL FASHION: MAGIC AND MYTHS

Fashion trends are like amorphous cloudy dreams, magical and mythical. For the novice it is a journey into fantasyland, of the sheers that Paris Hilton wears, or the printed scarf that Kate Moss throws casually around her shoulder. Here is an attempt to sift fact from fiction, myth from reality.

1) Black is beautiful, ever and forever!

Yes, black continues internationally to be the most solid and popular colour. Whilst it is commendable for formals in cold countries, it is certainly not optimum for tropical or warmer countries. Greys and browns, would be great in India, Singapore or Brazil. An entire industry has sprung up in the black colour, at the cost of other suitable colours like grey or blue.

Unfortunately, women too, have also fallen prey to the black brigade in all continents, irrespective of climate or culture. There is no need for women in Brazil or Peru to don black daily, when their countries have such vibrant orange and purple colours, as seen at their dances like the samba and salsa. The colour of clothes needs to compliment the best natural features of a person e.g. eye colour, skin tone and body shape. It does not have to be dictated by a fashion icon.

Former president aspirant, Madam Hillary Clinton, has been teased for choosing safe, solid colour pantsuits, by the fashion sorority in New York. Nevertheless, for a lady, who could have been the president of the most powerful democracy in the world, it was more important to appear to be firm, than to wear sparkling colours to appease fashion scribes.

2) Distress look is great!

It is common for the rich and famous to dress up in tattered clothes. Perhaps they are tired of being wealthy and wish to go back to their roots. Torn jeans, soiled, shrunk T-shirts and socks with holes are some of the arsenal of this fashion fraternity.

Some years ago, a leading Bollywood actor was waiting for a flight, in torn jeans and a dull T-shirt. An airport official, who had not heard about the 'Distress Look', walked up to me and said, "He dresses so well in the movies, and see how he looks in real life. I thought he is one of the highest paid actors in India. Why is he dressed up in torn jeans?" I explained to him the concept of the 'Distressed Look'. The man thought I was crazy. "I have spent my entire life getting away from rags to decent middle class clothing. Now the top stars are dressing up in torn clothes!" he retorted.

"This is fashion," I advised him! He thought I was pulling his leg.

3) Dressing down is good!

It is becoming plebeian for professionals to turn up for important meetings, in casual clothes like jeans. Their shirts hang outside the trousers. The casual look is designed to be 'cool', whatever that means. The tie seems to be exiting too.

Now, the way a man dresses for a meeting shows the importance of that convention. An assembly of people is held to achieve certain goals. Impressions do count. If a banker turns up for a convention unshaved and in jeans, then most people would be unlikely to trust him with their portfolios.

Men do look casual in official encounters, with open neck shirts and suits. Credibility improves if a formal jacket is accompanied by a tie, or at least a polo shirt. When you are too 'cool', you tell your client, his business does not matter to you. So, tattered jeans, with holes all over, are impasse at office meetings.

Dressing down may be fine when you visit your in-laws over the weekend, but not when you are bidding for a new account or if you are the President or Prime Minister of a country.

4) Designer, over-sized bags are a must:

Every couple of months, brands like Gucci and Louis Vuitton launch a new handbag, in limited numbers designed to make the famous seek these pieces. Then every fashion queen of the world from Naomi Campbell in London to Paris Hilton in New York to Mrs. Chopra in Mumbai or Mrs. Lalwani in Dubai, move heaven and earth to get the bag! The cost of manufacture of these bags would not be more than 30 to 40 per cent of the sales price. However, there is status and pride in being able to proclaim that you have the latest Gucci handbag.

Often these bags are desperately oversized. It just means that Madam Fashion has to carry extra weight. How many essential items does a woman really need to carry in her bag daily? Together they would not weigh more 300 grams to 400 grams. Yet, they carry handbags designed to haul one to two kilograms of cosmetics and accessories.

5) Accessories are vital, they are you:

Yes, the focus on accessories is perpetual. Fine accessories made from gold, platinum, silver, combined with precious and semi-precious stones and costume accessories made from low cost materials like metals with gold or silver finishes, wood, plastic and beads will continue to sway women. Costume jewellery is usually a combination of glass, synthetic or some semi-precious stones.

There is advice galore about 'wearing contrasting shapes if you have a round body build, ivory and tortoise shell, but only if they're fake'. There is much counsel about good, basic costume jewellery, pair of matching gold bangle bracelets, link necklaces in varying lengths, pair of simple gold hoop earrings, or gold button-style clip-ons, etc."

There will also be counsel about "buying a two-tone watch so that you can wear it with silver or gold jewellery, keeping your jewellery organised." There is much advice on what not to do also! "Never wear real and fake diamonds together, for it will make the real look fake! Pierce your ears more than twice in each lobe. However, never wear earrings so heavy that they stretch your lobes." Silver jewellery is of course impasse if your shirt or jacket has gold buttons.

This is all solid advice.

However recently I visited a lady CEO of a large corporation on work. She was dressed stylish in a jacket and trouser, but did not have a single piece of jewellery or ornament on her person. Yet, she radiated dignity and management power.

6) Wear tight fitting clothes that wrap around the body:

Fashion gurus advise avoidance of loose fitting clothes, which are baggy and could, make the wearer look sloppy. The perfect fit and look, is in.

Sure, clothes that wrap around the body are ideal. However, for people with large waists, it would make sense to wear trousers with pleats, or a double-breasted blazer, than a single-breasted one. What about a lady with rather large hips? A loose skirt would be more appropriate for her than a tight trouser.

The style gurus are advocating the use of sheer materials for dresses and blouses. The sleeves will receive special attention. Translucent sheers may not be too popular in conservative countries like India, Pakistan, UAE, etc.

Eventually, a smart person will study his or her body, and select clothes and designs, which supplement the body structure, rather than just buy apparel on the basis of current trends. You can add colour to your wardrobe, by donning a scarf print top or a silk scarf on a one-colour top as girls in Paris do so often.

7) Let your style and clothes talk:

It is trendy to deploy fashion for transmitting messages. Public messages, private messages and slogans are being broadcast through clothes. There are T-shirts, shirts with smiley faces, hearts, reindeers and animal prints embossed on them. There are girls wearing trousers with messages like 'Baby Doll', or 'Am good', 'Baby', etc., splashed on them. Some teenage girls wear T-shirts with messages like, 'Do you like me', or 'I am too good!'

It is better to be stylish and well dressed, than to use your wardrobe as an advertising hoarding. The most stylish jeans are not the widest or narrowest or hip hugging or rinsed; they're the ones that fit the best. To the lady with substance, whilst her hair style is important, it does not matter if it is the Bob, Razor Cut with Layers, Masculine, Soft Wedge Haircut, or Poker Straight.

Nor does it matter to the woman of substance that Shakira wore the fluid Carolina Herrera Resort Dress, when she attended the Herz fur Kinder charity telethon. And the fashion pundits debated whether the dress fitted, because she's not tall. Talented Shakira would get an audience, in any dress, anywhere, even in a canvas bag, because she is a radiant and energising personality.

A lady who dresses very simply and elegantly, and radiates serenity and power, is Mrs. Sonia Gandhi. No fancy brand names, no fashion icons around her. However, she always combines style with simplicity. Of course, she learnt much from her illustrious mother-in-law, Mrs. Indira Gandhi. Mrs. Indira Gandhi too dressed very simply, yet was always very classy.

8) All this Man and Woman stuff:

The last few years have seen the emergence of a unisex fashion market i.e. clothes, accessories that can be used by men or women. Bright and colourful shoes, garment trimmings and colossal sized sunglasses, have slipped in furtively into male fashion over the last few years, disguised as unisex colours or designs.

Some of the items for men are rather repulsive e.g. red designer jeans for men, or multi coloured night suits or pink coloured inner wear. Bright colours may be hot on women, but rarely look great on men. Again, men wearing sleeveless, coloured vests, on weekends to work, are taboo.

The unisex sunglass or belt is the product of the laziness of the designer. Fundamentally, men prefer strong designs and metallic colours. Women lean towards more colourful, softer designs and patterns. It is better to design fashion along these traditional lines, rather than creating indistinguishable merchandise.

Similarly, men in skinny jeans sporting jackets, is another forecast of unisex Fashion.

9) Bold is Beautiful:

The fashion pundits dictate that bold and defiant looks are in vogue. So, dare to be different in colour, styles, cuts and fabrics to be noted and honoured. Salma Hayek, Natalie Portman, Lucy Liu made heads turn in Hollywood, with their sheer necklines.

Yet, fashion is fundamentally about being comfortable with what you enjoy wearing, what makes you feel yourself and what makes you feel good. Eventually fashion is not merely about being different or standing out. It is about being yourself.

11

THE A, B, C, OF HUMAN RELATIONS IN RETAIL MANAGEMENT

A: ACCEPT genuinely, that 'Business is people 'and retail is about dealing with people i.e. customers, suppliers and ultimately, employees. Employees are the first customers of any retail business. If employees are disgruntled, they will not render good service to customers, vendors and suppliers. I have yet to see a prosperous retailer or a flourishing outlet, in London, Dubai, Sao Paulo and Mumbai, whose employees are melancholic.

B: BEHAVIOUR of the managers should demonstrate conviction of the people factor in retail management. Mission statements and words must be supported by action. People are not dumb, just because they do not possess an array of degrees. I have met sales staff on the floors that are sharper than managers. Due to economic reasons, they may not have been able to pursue higher studies. Their native intelligences are vibrant. Talent is desperately short in the world, and will continue to be so. So, we must respect and covet our people.

C: CUSTOMER-SERVICE is the soul of any retail outlet. If all the employees from top to bottom comprehend and believe in this concept passionately, the outlet will be the 'talk of the town'. Any retail outlet, ultimately sells, services and smiles.

D: DEVELOP leaders, everywhere! There is a leader in every sales girl, merchandiser or manager. (In a recent Hindi movie, a character pronounces, "There is a lion in everyone. It only needs someone to tickle it, to make it roar!") All work gets routine after some time. Then people get bored. They either commence job hunting or become disruptive. It is invigorating to develop leadership qualities in all mangers and promote from within when opportunities arise. Leadership qualities can be developed amongst team members through on-the-job training, classroom training and also counselling sessions.

E: ESTABLISH systems, manuals, procedures and business processes for all retail operations in rigorous detail. This will help to trim arbitrariness in the management of the store. Manuals also prescribe procedures, for standardisation of fundamentals across retail stores and branches. Lest we forget: Retail is Detail!

F: FORGE teams out of employees. Make each section, floor, category an independent unit, and foster team spirit by giving them collective tasks and team prizes for their achievements. Encourage the teams to spend informal times together i.e. a picnic, or a movie, and outing, to augment bonding.

G: GENERATE challenges to keep your high-fliers motoring in top gear. High-energy managers and staff live on very high energy levels. These high performance managers, need to kill a lion daily (i.e. manage a challenge daily). There is an element of routine in retail, which can lead to boredom. High performance staff has to be kept ceaselessly motivated through innovative concepts, ideas, rapid expansions and diversifications.

H: HELP your employees round the clock. If someone falls sick in the middle of the night, train your managers to land up at the employee's house to take him to the hospital or look after him. If an employee is going through some problem and seeks support, ensure that he receives some counselling from professionals. Dedicated and devoted teams are the result of the mindset of being a 'Help-Desk' to your employees.

I: INVOLVE your top management in key decisions pertaining to new concepts, expansions, diversifications and promotions of senior staff. Many entrepreneurs tend to take such decisions themselves. This can dampen the commitment and zeal of the top managers. They need to involve their senior teams in all major decisions to grow into great retailers.

J: JUDGE employees on pure merit. Retailers, who run their businesses professionally, flourish. Avoid favouritism and nepotism like the plague. In a family business make your sons and daughters labour their way, up the ladder, like a trainee. You will then teach them the best lessons of their lives. They will value this training even decades later. Their colleagues would also respect the professionalism in the company.

K: KNOWLEDGE is power in the retail business. Product knowledge is the key to excellent customer service. Employees should be updated constantly on new technologies, IT systems, selling techniques, etc. In a retail chain selling electronic products, the sales staff must understand the technical features and assist customers in smart decisions. When we were launching a mega hypermarket for electronics in the Middle East, we recruited the entire staff about 10 weeks in advance and trained them rigorously. Every salesman had to open the products they were going to sell i.e. a mobile or a camera, understand all the parts and then assemble the product.

L: LOSING a retail professional or team, built over the years, due to petty squabbling, ego-clashes or feeble remuneration, is unwise. Ordinary people, who work selflessly in a store, are the foundation of great retail businesses. It is vital to ensure that trained and committed staff are retained.

M: MOTIVATE teams for superior performance through personal encouragement, financial rewards, status enhancement, sales contests, bonuses, so that teams feel invigorated and appreciated. Ensure that staff gets an adequate monthly salary to live decently, i.e. a fixed salary of 70 per cent of the total package and the balance through incentives.

N: NICETIES are important. Never ever condone the use of foul language or uncouth manners on the shop floors. Chewing of gum, winking, scratching, talking on the mobile, etc., is highly obnoxious to customers. Appoint a floor-coach in every outlet, who will focus on etiquette of the staff.

O: 'OUTPERFORM targets' culture! Encourage your team, so that they do not just meet targets, but exceed them. Teams must be willing to do that little incremental walk, that extra mile to meet goals. Delivering beyond the normal call of duty makes the difference between a competent retail outlet or a great retail outlet.

P: PROFITS are crucial to a retail business. Without profits, no business can survive. However, profits augment if the habit of thinking profits is inculcated down the line. Directors, managers, staff or watchmen must all think profits. Margins are principally low in retail; hence costs have to be watched like hawks at all levels.

Q: QUIET periods, whereby senior managers get away from the daily store pressures, once a quarter help to generate new ideas. So, have a 'blue-sky' day, debating innovations and improvements. This will yield many practical ideas for operational efficiencies. It will also bond team members.

R: REMUNERATING the team judiciously is a key element of retailing. If a retailer pays employees below their market value, they will depart. It takes time and money to recruit and train new staff.

S: SALARY reviews, comparisons with competitors are vital to ensure that staff is remunerated competitively. This will also contribute to retaining the team.

T: TRAINING and development of the staff on a continuous basis, brings latest management practices into the retail group and also motivates the staff. Top team members must be sensitised to dealing with the government and local authorities.

U: UNDERSTAND the customers, via the floor staff, by spending time with them in the shops. Sales staffs on the floors are brilliant sources of information about customer preferences. These insights are free.

V: VERY important it is, for top management to interact with the Governments to explicate the advantages of large formats of retail for India for employment generation and tax revenues. Retailing in India is nascent. There are social concerns to be addressed by senior managers.

W: WEE extra benefits like a meal scheme, transportation from and to the residence, when the workplace is far away, make a massive difference to the morale of a team at negligible costs.

X: X-RAYABLE, transparent operations, invariably ensure respect from employees. A transparently managed retail business, that pays taxes, adheres to labour laws, pays its employees on time and stands glued to its word, lures the best talent.

Y: YOURS is the whole retail world, if you can adhere to this list, build a team, which respects the values enshrined in the ethical practices of the company.

Z: ZEBRA Crossing Line: The personal life of employees is akin to a Zebra crossing line in HR. Frequently employers have a habit of getting embroiled in the personal lives of their employees, which is avoidable. Employers should respect the 'Zebra Line', to forge a strong team.

12

QUOTES AND DISCUSSIONS: RAJENDRA ANEJA ON MODERN RETAIL

1) Quoted in a Book on 'INDIA'S STORE WARS – Retail Revolution and the Battle for the Next 500 Million Shoppers'. By Mr. Geoff Hiscock

"A long-time participant in and observer of the Indian retail scene, Rajendra K. Aneja, believes employers must infuse "a passion for success" among their staff. Aneja, a former managing director of Unilever Tanzania and now CEO of the industrial business of Switz Group in Dubai – part of Switz India – says staff who are company employees, rather than being outsourced from agencies, will have greater commitment. He also urges retailers to make every employee a partner through a stock options scheme. "A watchman who knows that he has a stake in the final profits, in the form of a bonus or a stock option, will ensure zero level of shrinkage." Aneja says that astute retailers will look after the health and wellbeing of their staff, providing good meals, washrooms and restrooms. They will train them continuously, and they will motivate them not just with money, but with respect, a career path and a sense that they are part of a family. Staff training, he says, is a retailer's best investment. As Aneja says, retailers have to accept the fact that skills are scarce. Even when the talent pool is one billion-plus Indians, it always makes sense to hang onto good staff."

2) FROM RETAILWIRE (March 2008)

"The politics of organised retail will be short-lived" by Rajendra Aneja
Eight expert Comments

GLOBAL BUSINESS INDIA METRO
Excerpt of an article from *Indiaretailing.com*, presented here for discussion.

"The time for retailing in India, as an organised industry, has arrived. The government should immediately permit FDI (foreign direct investment) in retail. This will encourage large retailers like Metro, Tesco and Carrefour to get serious about their India plans. The entry of these international players will usher in a new paradigm in retailing in India.

Retail is poised to be one of the largest employment avenues in India. This will enable provisions of various industrial and labor laws to be applied to the retail industry also, which will help to manage businesses more pragmatically and systematically. Modern trade, in terms of hypermarkets/supermarkets, also improves the quality of service and augments the range of products to consumers. A store like Ikea offers thousands of economically priced products, including furniture and storage spaces, which can revolutionise daily living for the middle and lower income segments of our society.

Organised retail currently constitutes only two to three percent of the retail business in India. Thus, the dreaded phantom of swamping by large retailers is a figment of imagination.

Certainly, there will be a fallout. The smaller and marginal outlets will be impacted, and the more incompetent ones may have to shift to other businesses. But then, India abounds in opportunities.

Even in many second-world countries like Indonesia, Brazil, Venezuela, Colombia and Saudi Arabia, which abound with international hypermarkets, about 50 to 70 percent of the groceries, vegetable and fruit trade takes place through the traditional stores.

So, hypermarkets and malls will not sound the death-knell for small stores. In fact, many small stores flourish more, because their sales increase. Customers do not visit hypermarkets at the drop of a hat. A visit to a large store has to be planned. For daily grocery purchases, consumers continue to visit the corner shop. Interestingly, with the arrival of modern retailing and hypermarkets, the smaller neighborhood stores invariably spruce up in terms of layout, hygiene, merchandising and customer service.

Thus, the entire trade becomes more hygiene- and customer-conscious.

Modern retailing as exemplified through supermarkets and hypermarkets is an imminent phase in India. It can be delayed, not stopped. The government should facilitate it. Why should a billion-strong population not have the freedom of choice, which is the essence of democracy?"

Discussion Questions: What do you think of the opportunity for American retailers to expand into India? Is the Indian government justified in their caution concerning a possible adverse affect on smaller stores? How do you think expansion into India might differ from past efforts to expand into regions such as Brazil, China or Mexico?

COMMENTS:

Comment 1.

Lee Peterson
EVP Brand, Strategy & Design, WD Partners

There is no doubt that there is an opportunity for American retailers in India, but for indications as to how large or better yet, how fast, take a look at what's already there compared to China. China is eons ahead.

However, we believe that, given the right set of circumstances, including arrangements with local retailers and officials, the opportunity is still immense. But perhaps more importantly, it could potentially be bigger for Indian retailers in the short AND long run. Operations like IndiaBulls have shown a propensity to create inviting retail propositions for a consumer they understand much better than American retailers do and will therefore move much quicker in establishing a presence.

It should be a very exciting and very competitive environment going forward.

Comment 2.

Max Goldberg
President, Max Goldberg & Associates

Any major potential paradigm shift is bound to be cautiously considered. The Indian government is being cautious about letting foreign retailers, particularly hypermarkets and supermarkets, into the country.

Retailers should also proceed cautiously. As Carrefour discovered in Mexico and Japan, and Wal-Mart discovered in Germany, retailing outside your home country is not as simple as building and stocking stores. Besides employing real estate and demographic experts, they should hire sociologists to understand how the local people think.

India is a huge potential market. It should be open to foreign retailers. But both the country and the retailers should proceed judiciously.

Comment 3.

Doron Levy

India can be called the next China in terms of economic growth. Simply put, no amount of government intervention will stop the ball rolling. Right now, India is a retail mosaic, littered with small independents with no real consistency. This situation makes it ripe for a large format brand to step in and create a new marketplace. Can Americans succeed in India? Depends on whether they will embrace national and local cultural differences.

I use our communities here in the Greater Toronto Area as a reference point. Many large chains develop local store marketing initiatives that are directed to the diversity within the community they serve. American chains will have to do something different than their European counterparts. But overall the market in India is ready for some big players.

Comment 4.

Tom Thurow

Undoubtedly, the opportunity for organised retail in India is tremendous. Whether it will rival China remains to be seen.

There remain hurdles with government, local business pressures, cultural shift requirements and infrastructure.

Having worked and lived in India for an Indian retailer, I submit there are no international retailers that can "set up shop" without understanding there will be a HUGE expense to develop passable national highways and world class distribution facilities.

The "cost of entry" goes beyond opening stores.

Comment 5.

Jerry Tutunjian

For years India had a commendable policy of self-sufficiency–everything from old Humbers (renamed Ambassador) to film for photography to soft drinks were all made domestically. However, the retail section was mired in the '20s, if not earlier.

I think Indian consumers are eager to welcome Western products, services, retail channels, etc. Besides, some 80 million are considered middle class–they earn a healthy salary, are "westernised" and highly educated. There's lots of opportunity for U.S. exporters in India, now and in the long-distance future.

MY EXPERIENCES IN MODERN RETAIL

Comment 6.

Pradip V. Mehta, P.E.

There are ample opportunities for American retailers in India provided they offer "American" products and not run of the mill consumer products made in China. Products and companies like Apple, Dell, Nike, etc. have huge potential because American products and designs are considered aspirational and status symbols.

Comment 7.

Devangshu Dutta
Interesting topic.

The so-called "politics of organised retailing" are no different from the politics of anything. There are interest-groups and pressure-groups with different objectives, who pull-and-push economic and regulatory policy with varying degrees of success. In that, India is no different from any other country, whether the US or China.

After China began opening up its economy in 1979, it took more than a decade for it to begin allowing foreign retailers to enter the market, and it was not before domestic retailers were given time to scale up.

Even in the US of current times, there are places which would be up in arms at the whiff of a Wal-Mart store proposal.

As we discuss today, in the UK the Competition Commission is preparing a report on how retail consolidation is affecting the sector and the consumer.

So the answer to the question about "the politics of organised retail" is: yes, there is politics involved, and if you are an interested party then there is no option but to be part of the politics.

While on the issue about opportunities in the Indian market, I'm reminded of a couple of conversations, one with a client and another with an associate, who compared the Indian market to the US and the UK, respectively, in the 1970s.

My response to them, and to the question above, is: yes, there is tremendous opportunity in India now, as there was in those markets in the 1970s. Yes, in parts the market, the distribution structure etc. may remind you of the US and the UK in the 1970s. But to assume that it will play out the same way would be dangerous.

There are many other cultural, economic and social factors, apart from the infrastructure, to take into account.

My advice: approach India as India in the 2008, don't approach it as the US in the 1970s. Or as China, Brazil or Mexico.

Comment 8.

Mark Lilien

When well-capitalised skillful players enter Indian retailing, they will destroy many mom and pop "stores". In many cases, those "stores" are simple peddlers selling their wares at the side of the road. India wants to maximise employment. There's a trade-off between allowing every possible form of competition and maximising employment. A new Wal-Mart might employ 300 people but put 1,000 peddlers out of business. India is a socialist country trying to minimise economic strife. Unlimited free retail competition maximises economic strife.

PHOTOGRAPHS, PART II

Photograph 21: High Street shopping in Boston (USA).

Photograph 22: High Street shop, Boston (USA).

Photograph 23: Modern Retail is becoming popular in developing countries in Africa. A supermarket in Tanzania.

Photograph 24: Malls have to generate excitement to lure visitors. A fashion show in a mall in Dubai.

Photograph 25: An attraction to amuse children in a mall in the UAE.

Photograph 26: The Abu Dhabi Municipality has encouraged small grocery shops to modernise and maintain high levels of hygiene.

MY EXPERIENCES IN MODERN RETAIL

Photograph 27: A large upscale mall in Pune, India.

Photograph 28: The Weekly Fiera market in Sao Paulo, Brazil, selling local handicrafts.

Photograph 29: The Weekly Fiera market in Sao Paulo, Brazil, selling Brazilian paintings.

Photograph 30: The weekly Fiera Market in Sao Paulo, Brazil, Refreshments for shoppers.

SECTION II

13

HOW TO START A NEW RETAIL CONCEPT STORE? THE NUTS AND BOLTS

A. Developing the Concept and Starting:

1. Value proposition:

It is very important to have comprehensive clarity about the benefits that the customer will derive by visiting the Store. Store management must ceaselessly ask, "Why should a customer visit our outlet?" Customers always seek best value and a great deal.

Some of the elements of the value proposition are best price, widest range, excellent service, technical advice, etc. Customers visit stores for solutions to problems. The Store management has to be clear what consumer needs will be fulfilled.

2. Market segmentation:

The retailer needs to identify the segment of the market that will be catered to. The market should be segmented by income, age, price, values, etc. If the Store is going to sell homecare products, the market will principally comprise of women, more specifically housewives. Identifying the clusters of customers, who will be the primary market for the Store, will contribute to offering products which will be appreciated and purchased by the consumer.

3. Theme of the Store:

An outlet should have an overriding theme, which helps to identify the Store and its products. For instance, a Store selling gardening equipment may have a Green earth theme. The Store would then have green as the predominant colour in it, including the furniture, uniforms, etc.

4. Ambience:

The ambience of the Store should reflect the theme and segment of the market being catered to. Ambience is a blend of many factors and creates a mood in the outlet. The colours of the Store, the lighting deployed and the displays should all blend to create a certain atmosphere. For instance, one would never use tube lights in a premium Store in a mall. The look and feel of the Store impacts its perception and the footfalls.

5. Destination Store or 'me too':

Is the Store envisaged to be the largest and most comprehensive Store in town, where a customer can buy all that he needs for the house? A large range or assortment can lead to the reputation of being a 'Destination Store'. For instance, a newly married couple can just go to Ikea in Dubai and buy their requirements of a new apartment, ranging from beds to lamps to pots and pans in just one day. Ikea is clearly a destination store.

6. Category killer:

Does the retailer want to create a category killer, i.e. the best store in a particular product group or it is the intention to just be another successful player in the cluster? Many destination stores could also be classified as category killers.

7. Budget for Store:

Every business venture begins with a budget, an estimate of the total monies required for the project. It is vital to construct a budget for the Store, at the commencement stage. There is no point in trying to create a category killer store, if the budgets are limited. Budgets should also provide for contingencies and overruns on time schedules.

8. Meeting with CEOs:

It is useful to meet the CEOs of the group's other retail businesses and get their views on the new concepts being planned by the company. If the other CEOs have a retail background, they may have bright ideas to offer. If a business group is engaged in retailing of foods and apparel and is now planning to enter furniture retailing, it would be useful to get the CEOs of the foods and apparel businesses to opine on the new venture. They may be new to the furniture business, but they do understand retailing.

B. Agreements and Understandings:

9. Board members, on board:

The promoters should organise meetings with all the Board members or stakeholders to ensure agreement to the new Store concepts and budgets.

10. Permissions and meetings - Government, local authorities:

If any permissions are required from the government or municipal authorities, it is best to get them early enough to save time.

11. Terms and conditions:

If the retail Store is being created on a franchisee basis it is important to understand all the provisions and clauses in detail. What are the provisions regarding sharing of profits and costs? Who will select the design of the Store, the fitments, etc.? Who will be responsible for training and development of the staff, the visuals, publicity, etc.? The Agreement with the franchiser should be studied rigorously.

12. Rentals of property:

The rentals quoted for the Store by leaser should be crosschecked with prevailing market rates in the neighbourhood and in other malls of the same category. In case of outright purchase of the property also, the prevailing market prices must be determined. The estimates of inflationary trends in property prices and rates should also be factored. It is beneficial to have a property consultant advising on this.

13. Basis of rentals - flat rent, or per cent of sales:

Mall owners charge a flat rental or they charge a rental on the basis of per cent of the sales of the outlet or a mix of both. The exact provisions have to be studied in detail and then a final view should be taken.

14. Number of years' agreement, lock-in period, etc.:

It is useful to clarify for how many years the Store can be based in the location. What are the provisions for extending the lease and on what conditions? Is there a rent escalation clause? It is inconvenient to move the Store every five or ten years. If the Store does well, the landlord may wish to escalate the rentals or demand that you vacate. Thus, it is important that there are adequate safeguards to protect the Store space. It is best to seek legal ratification on these issues. The lock-in period from both the sides also needs to be determined and included in the agreement. A lock-in from the lessor may be sought for the entire lease period, to avoid any problems later.

15. Possibilities of renewal or extension:

It is important to ensure that there are adequate provisions to protect the rights to get renewals and extensions of lease, in the agreement. The renewal of the lease must be done sufficiently in advance, e.g. in case of a five-year lease, the renewal agreement may be signed a year in advance of the expiry of the lease, say for another term of five years. The negotiations for the renewal may require another two to three months, prior to signing of the renewal agreement. In case the lease is not renewed, one has to procure new retail premises and shift operations. This will impact the business, if not planned in advance.

16. Refining the agreements:

The draft agreements with the franchiser should also be discussed with a local lawyer or legal team of the retailer, to understand any underlying nuances or implications. A stitch is better than nine, so it is best to clear all doubts early enough, to avoid any heartburn or legal disputes at a later stage when the business has commenced.

17. Franchiser - Policies on returns, display support, etc.:

The policies of the franchiser regarding return of unsold stocks, damages, etc. should be clarified in the Franchise agreement. It is also prudent to clarify the type and quantum of support that the franchiser will provide for displays, merchandising, etc.

18. Franchiser - Training and development:

Some franchisers also provide training to the staff of the franchisee in the Store or at their headquarters. This arrangement needs to be clarified.

19. Signing of agreements, disputes:

It is important to check where the agreement has to be signed in case the franchiser is based in another country. The provisions pertaining to the country where issues have to be legally managed should also be very clear. Suppose the arrangement with a franchiser in the USA turns sour for some reason at a later stage, a retailer based in Mumbai or Dubai could get saddled with legal cases abroad.

C. Location:

20. Mall or High Street?

The retailer has to take a fundamental decision as to whether the new Store will be based in a mall or on the High Street. If the plan is to open the new Store at multiple locations, it would be provident to have presence in the malls and also the High Streets.

21. Floor of the mall:

If the Store is to be based in a mall, it should ideally be located on the ground floor or the first floor. Customer traffic is lower on the upper floors of a mall, unless a very important destination Store is located there. As a general rule, the ground floor location is the best.

22. Neighbouring stores:

Neighbours are very important at home and at work. Whether the Store is based in a mall or on the High Street, try to ensure that the neighbouring outlets have some congruence to the new product concept. So if the proposed Store is selling fashion garments, try to locate in the fashion arena and avoid being next to an electronics store. Similarly, in the High Street avoid being next to a low-end restaurant.

23. Proximity to entrance, restaurants or movie theatres:

In determining the exact location of the new Store in a mall, it is valuable to study the flow of traffic. A location at the entrance, near the restaurant or movies area, where the traffic flow is high will be preferable. Locations at the exit are avoidable, since the shoppers are in a dash to depart. Generally, malls earmark specific zones for fashion outlets, home products outlets, restaurants, entertainment, etc.

D. Constructing the Store:

24. Finalise architect:

The architect to be appointed should have experience in retail and fashion in the local country but also abroad. He should understand shopper behaviour, traffic flows of customers and the nuances of retailing in a variety of products. It is important to be bold and innovate. Consider an architect who specialises in fashion to design a new consumer durables Store. Be bold and daring. The cross fertilisation may result in a masterpiece Store. If the Store is under a franchisee arrangement, it is possible that the franchiser may recommend an architect.

25. Drawings:

The architect should submit detailed Store drawings. Some architects furnish 50 drawings for a 15,000 square foot store; other architects may submit over 500 drawings for the same store. Consider the architect who provides over 500 detailed drawings, so that all facets of the Store will be clear to the construction contractor.

26. Construction contractor:

The contractor should ideally be a person or party who is either known to Store management or has excellent references. He should have some experience in constructing retail outlets.

27. Scope of work:

The responsibilities of the architect and the contractor should be clearly delineated to avoid any confusion at a later stage.

28. Penalty clauses:

It is vital to ensure that there are adequate penalty clauses in the agreements with the architect and contractor, in case there are delays in the execution of the project. Contractors are not uniformly efficient on delivery, across countries. Moreover, the penalty clauses should be tough enough for the contractor to put his shoulder to the wheel and get the Store ready on schedule.

29. Range of materials and specifications:

The range of materials to be used in building the entire Store and the specifications should be clearly incorporated in the drawings from the architect and the agreement with the contractor.

30. Introduction fees – architects:

Some architects charge an introduction fee when they introduce their clients to contractors and even fitment suppliers. There should be a clear understanding whether such fees will be paid, the basis and the quantum.

31. Segmentation of the Store by product category:

Before the drawings are initiated, the specific segment of the market, which the Store will cater to, should be clear and should be elucidated to the architect and the contractor. The ambience and manifestation of an outlet selling premium fashion apparel, is very different from an outlet selling casual apparel. The segment of the market being catered to impacts the entire Store design.

32. Any shop-in-shop possibilities:

If the plan is to have some small shops in the main Store, then this concept should be incorporated at the design stage itself, so that the space can be provided in the drawings. e.g. an electronics brand such as Apple or Samsung may wish to set up a 250 to 500 square feet shop in the large outlets of an electronics retail chain.

33. Locating various categories:

In a large multi-product outlet, the layout of the various categories in the Store, should principally be determined by customer convenience and flow. For instance, in any supermarket, fresh vegetables and fruits are purchased most frequently. So, these convenience items should be located in the proximity of the entrance of the store. Many customers visit a supermarket three to four times a week, just to purchase their requirements of fresh vegetables and fruits. There is no point in making such customers walk through the entire store each time. I have visited a large supermarket in Kampala, Uganda, where the fresh foods are sold on the first floor. So a shopper has to walk through the entire store and climb stairs to buy vegetables. Why should she do so? She will prefer to shop a neighbourhood store.

Similarly, in a multi-brand electronic store, mobile phones and cameras are the most purchased items. It is sound logic to have the counters of these two categories near the entrance of the store.

34. Space for advertising:

Whilst designing the Store it is useful to earmark areas, walls, etc. which will be principally deployed for permanent advertising for the Store brand name. If the Store is envisaged to be a multi-brand Store, e.g. Croma or Vijay Sales electronics store, then these spaces can be even rented to other companies to generate incremental revenues.

35. Space for promotions and merchandisers:

Supermarkets generally have promoters from suppliers engaged in promotional activities. Adequate space should be provided for sales promoters and promotions at the architect's drawing stage. Customers find it irritating when they push their trolleys in crowded aisles, to bump against sales promoters sampling a mayonnaise or a marmalade.

36. Number of cash tills:

The architect must specify the number and location of the cash tills in the Store early enough. The cash tills should be so located to facilitate convenience of payment. However, the location of the cash tills should not prevent free flow of customers in the shopping areas.

37. Planning and installing public address system:

A professional store should have a public address system. This will help the store management to communicate with the shoppers and also with staff members, as required. The number of speakers should be determined in advance so that they can be incorporated into the ceilings or walls.

38. Music in Store:

The Store has to have music playing in it for the entertainment of the customers. It is necessary to finalise the system and the place where the music system will be kept. Ideally it should be kept discreetly at the reception or in the back area of the Store.

The music played should be in keeping with the tenor of the Store and the tastes of the customers. Now this can be a challenge in a Store in an international city like Dubai, Singapore or London. Customers from a range of countries visit the Stores. How does the Store keep everyone entertained? It is safe to play music from a range of countries in instrumental form. Music should be varied depending on any predominant festival e.g. Diwali, Christmas, New Year, etc.

E. Selection of Floors, Ceiling and Lights:

39. Tiles and Lights: Designs and patterns:

The designs and patterns of the tiles and the lights to be used in the Store (including the ceiling), should be determined in consultation with the architect. It is useful to visit the market to see the latest offerings and also study catalogues from local and overseas manufacturers.

40. Use of interior and external lights:

Lights are a very crucial factor in a retail store. The lights to be deployed at various spots, in all the sections, should be finalised in consultation with the architect.

41. Intensity of lights:

The intensity of the light can be varied to highlight the features or the characteristics of a product. The type and quantum of light on a product or brand, determines it focus and even consumer reactions.

42. Colours of lights:

It needs to be checked with the mall authorities whether they have any preferences about the colour of the lights to be used in all the outlets. Generally, they would prefer the same colour in all the shops.

43. Imported or locally available:

It is important to check whether the tiles are available locally or will have to be imported, since this will impact the time schedule.

44. Price and quality comparisons:

When all the material requirements for the Store have been finalised, it is necessary to check the prices, grades and qualities by obtaining a minimum of three quotations.

45. Lead times:

The lead times in the delivery of various construction materials should also be considered, since it will impact the schedule to complete the Store.

46. Selection of vendors:

The selection of vendors for supplies of the various materials can be left entirely to the architect and/or the building contractor, or the client may like to be involved in the process. It is useful for the client to be involved in these details.

47. Determining prices, terms and penalty clauses:

Ideally it is best for the building contractor to work through details of prices, terms and penalty clauses with various vendors e.g. plumbers, electricians, civil contractors, etc.

Contractors work with the same parties on many projects. They come with a team. If there is a binding contract with the building contractor with suitable penalty clauses, then it is best to give free space to the contractor to deliver the Store.

F. Fitments:

   48.   Types and range desired:

Deciding on the type of fitments, the range and the quantities for displaying the merchandise involves exploration and study. Novel fitments are being constantly innovated. It is useful to establish contacts with the top fitments providers and review their full range. The architect should also be involved in the selection process.

   49.   Quantities and numbers:

The architect and fitment supplier should provide guidance about the number of fitments required for different sections of the Store, depending on the products being merchandised and displayed. If the Store is being constructed for a franchiser, the latter is likely to provide guidelines about the type and numbers of fitments.

   50.   Local or imported:

It is advantageous to explore fitments manufacturers abroad in Italy, Germany, Japan, China, etc., depending on the budgets for the Store. It is not enough to study catalogues. It is worth the money to travel to these countries and see the fitments and the manufacturing facilities of the supplier.

51. Manufacturing material:

Fitments are available in a range of materials. The type of merchandise being sold is a key determinant of the type of materials for fitments. Here again, the advice of the architect is valuable.

52. Colours:

The colours of the fitments should blend with the overall Store colour and ambience. The architect should advise on the ideal blend of colours of the fitments. All colours in the Store should underscore the branding of the outlet.

53. Pricing:

Fitment budgets should be finalised after obtaining quotations from three to five vendors. The lowest cost estimate need not be the best; a qualitative and quantitative assessment is crucial. Hence, visits to the fitments suppliers are useful.

54. Lead period for delivery:

There should be clarity about the lead times for deliveries of the fitments, for they will have to be factored into the overall Store schedule.

G.   Branding and Signages:

55. Name of the Store:

The name of the Store has to be decided in consultation with the promoters and top management. Ideally the name of the Store should reflect the concept. A store name like Reliance Digital denotes that it is a store with digital and electronic products. A store name like Happy Homes, implies a store selling furniture and household products.

56. High visibility spots for Store name:

A list of high visibility spots has to be prepared in the Store where the name will be placed. These spots will certainly be at the entrances of the Store, but will also be at a few spots within the Store. The sizes of these high visibility spots should also be identified, for they will impact the size of the letterings and logos.

57. High visibility areas and lighting:

The important visibility spots in the Store should have extra lighting focussed on these areas. Lighting can enable enhanced focus on the product and the mood of the customer.

58. Approved designs, formats and scripts:

The design of the letters of the Store brand name should be decided in consultation with the architect. The exact themes and fonts of the alphabets should also be decided.

59. Approved logos:

It is necessary to ensure that all logos in the Store are legally cleared for use. These could be logos of the Store itself or those of the vendors whose products are to be sold.

60. Colours:

The colours of the various alphabets should be finalised to harmonise with the overall colour scheme of the Store. The architect should also advise on the colour scheme.

61. Registration of names, logos, in zones, countries, etc.

The brand name of the Store, the logos, etc. should be registered in all the countries in which the company may gradually launch the Store.

62. Check local languages translations:

If the name of the Store is being displayed in some local languages, it is important to get the local translations cleared from a language specialist. Sometimes language translation can be complex; hence it is important to get more than one specialist to give his views.

63. Visiting Card formats and branding:

The store should have a standard Visiting Card format for all the employees. The Visiting Card should carry the logo of the Store and also, if possible, the key value proposition of the

Store. The visiting card should also be used to strengthen the brand equity of the Store.

64. Deploy invoice to underscore branding and logo:

The invoice is a free branding opportunity. Besides providing the mandatory details of the purchase transaction, it should also be adroitly used to advertise the Store, its logo and its value proposition. The website, invoices, shopping bags, etc. should all be synchronised in terms of branding and colour schemes.

H. Visuals in Store:

65. Concepts:

The Store should be inviting and eye-catching for customers to want to walk into it, to see the merchandise and then perhaps buy it. The visual appearance of the Store should reflect the concept of the store. The store should have a formal look, if it is designed to sell formal office clothing for men. If it is selling casual apparel like jeans, it should have a youthful, brighter and colourful visualisation. Fundamentally the external visualisation should reflect the basic concept and tenor of the Store.

66. Location spots:

The spaces inside the Store where the visuals (product displays, etc.) are going to be placed should be clearly earmarked. Whilst these spots or areas should have high visibility, they should not obstruct the free flow of customers in the aisles.

67. Exact sizes of windows and displays:

The number and sizes of the various show windows at the entrance of the Store or in the other parts should be determined. Displays and visuals should be designed for all the windows and visual areas.

68. Renting of windows and visual spaces to maximise revenues:

Display windows and visual spaces can also be loaned to suppliers for highlighting their products. For instance, in an electronics store, vendors like Panasonic, Sony, LG, etc. would look forward to hiring the display areas for short periods of time to display their products.

69. Content of Visuals - Product, visuals, displays and materials:

The display windows, especially at the entrance should sum up the concept and the offering of the Store. The display and show windows should comprise of the products, merchandising materials, etc., to make them vibrant and captivating. They should compel the visitor to step into the Store.

70. Changing visuals:

The visuals and displays in the show windows and the Store should be changed at frequent intervals i.e. a fortnight to a month. Customers weary of the same displays quickly. It is important to kindle their interest continuously and ensure frequent visits. Making the Store vibrant by changing displays and visuals with new merchandise can lure customers.

71. Breaking monotony:

Visuals and show windows can also be placed within the Store at vantage points, to break the monotony of walking through aisles of stocks.

72. Use of flowers:

Flowers can be used adroitly to enhance the beauty of a Store. The supermarket chain Pau de Acucar in Brazil uses flowers very elegantly to enhance the beauty of its supermarkets. Granted, that the flowers are also for sale but their imaginative deployment enhances the stores.

73. Internal or external management:

A fundamental decision that Store management has to take is whether the visual management of the Store will be the responsibility of an in-house team in the Store, or will it be outsourced to an external agency. This would depend on the number of outlets that the company has. If there are a large number of outlets in the portfolio of the promoters, it would make eminent sense to have an in-house visualisation team.

However, if there are only two or three outlets to manage, then it may be provident to work with an external visualisation team.

I. Displays and merchandising:

74. Areas of displays and merchandising:

The areas of displays and merchandising of products in the Store should be clearly earmarked.

75. Responsibilities for merchandising and displays:

The overall responsibility for merchandising and displays should ideally be that of the Store manager. Even when there are multiple Stores and a team of visualisers has overall responsibility for displays, the concerned Store manager should be accountable for the displays.

76. Maintenance and cleaning of showcases:

The showcases in the Store should be cleaned regularly and should be well maintained. Any scratches, paint peeling, etc., should be attended to immediately. No item in the Store should ever look shoddy.

77. Policy on posters:

The Store management needs to have a clear policy whether it will permit posters to be placed in the premises for promotion of products. Ideally, posters should be avoided in the Stores.

78. Frames for posters and announcers:

If posters do have to be placed in the Store for some time to make some announcements, etc. they should ideally be framed.

79. Discussions with vendors for participation in displays, etc.:

In a multiproduct outlet like a supermarket or an electronics store, vendors would be very keen to hire extra spaces, shelves, merchandising spots for displaying their products and making them stand out. These discussions should commence almost six months before the opening of the Store since they can be time consuming.

80. Charges or fees for space and promotions in Store:

The charges and fees for listing, shelving, merchandising, displays, show windows renting, etc. should be finalised internally before commencing discussions with the vendors.

81. Rotation of Product displays:

Displays of products should be rotated at frequent intervals, i.e. weekly or fortnightly.

82. Placement of screens:

Large screens can be placed at strategic positions in the Store, for constantly advertising and screening commercials of products. The exact location of screens in the Store should be determined in advance. Ideally these TV sets should be on mute throughout.

83. Carry bags of products: material, colours and printed matter:

The carry bags for packing products are a powerful advertising medium. They can be used for branding the Store, detailing the various branches and highlighting some key features. However, it is important to avoid cluttering the carry bags with messages.

There should be a dominant colour of the carry bags, to make them identifiable even in the streets or malls. For instance, Oxford Street and Marble Arch streets literally turn green with crowds of shopper carrying the green shopping bags of Marks & Spencer.

84. Product catalogues:

Product catalogues should be detailed and professionally produced. They should also be updated at periodic intervals or at every new season, to keep the customers updated about the latest available collections.

J. Merchandise:

85. List of suppliers:

The Board or the CEO of the Store should approve the list of vendors. This should be done at least six months before the Store is scheduled to commence operations, so that there is adequate lead-time to order and receive inventories.

86. Agreements with vendors:

Agreements should be signed with the vendors who will supply stocks to the Store. The agreement should cover all the terms of the business including payment period, goods to be returned policies, etc.

87. Lead times:

The lead-time required by the vendors to make supplies should be clearly established.

88. List of merchandise:

At least six to eight weeks before the commencement of the Store the list of merchandise to be stocked should be ready and orders should be placed with the vendors. The specific orders, quantities, ranges, etc. should be discussed with the vendors too, in case they have any suggestions.

89. Date expiry stocks – timings of supply

Products, which have a date expiry period, like food products in a supermarket should be treated as a separate category. There should be clear understanding with the suppliers regarding stocks, which are unsold and date expired.

90. Placement of stocks on shelves, replenishments, etc.:

Some companies position their own merchandiser or salesman at the supermarket or multi-brands stores. The responsibility for placement of the products on the shelves, replenishments and rotation of stocks, is taken over by the vendor company. However, this is customary only for large companies selling fast moving consumer products. The accountability for stock management on the shelves should be clear i.e. is it that of the Store or the suppliers.

91. Inventory management in store and warehouse:

It is indeed dreadful to visit a supermarket and find some stocks missing from the shelves. So, at the time of agreeing the terms with the vendors, it should be clarified who has the responsibility for ensuring that the shelves are always well stocked. Is the responsibility that of the Store management or that of the vendor? The level of stocks to be maintained in the warehouse of the Store should also be specified. An out of stock position, in any store is a cardinal sin.

92. Monthly and quarterly stock audits:

A monthly and quarterly audit should be undertaken of all physical stocks in the Store and the warehouses to make sure that the physical and book stocks match.

93. Payment period:

The credit periods, payment terms and discounts on timely payments should be clearly stated in the agreements with the vendors.

94. Returns policy:

Stocks may get damaged during delivery, transhipment or handling. Whether the vendor accepts these stocks as returns, should be clarified.

K. Customer Service:

95. Corporate statement:

The corporate statement or mission statement or the basic consumer promise of the Store should be summarised in one line of about 10 to 12 words.

96. Space for corporate statement:

The statement should be displayed prominently in the Store, ideally near the entrance area of the Store or at the checkout area. All floor employees must be familiar with the corporate statement and should understand it clearly

97. Welcome – Signage:

There should be a signage welcoming customers to the Store at the entrance. The customer should be treated like an honoured guest visiting a home.

98. Thanks – Signage:

There should a signage thanking the customer for having visited the Store, at the exit. The signage should also state that the Store looks forward to the next visit of the customer.

99. Store locator:

If the Store is in a mall, it is useful to ensure that the store locater at the reception area clearly shows the location of the Store.

100. Category locator:

Within the Store, the various categories of products should be logically arranged and clearly indicated through signages, so that customers do not struggle to find the products they need to buy. Hypermarkets and stores are becoming very large sized abroad. Sometimes customers have a tough time finding the products that have come to shop. Hence adequate signages can be very helpful to customers.

101. Advisors and product consultants:

If the Store is selling technical or electronic products, the staff should be trained to help the customers to decide which features they need in their products and which models and brands will meet their requirements. The staff would have to be trained for this role.

102. Greeters at entrances:

It is a fantastic feeling for customers to be welcomed by greeters at the entrance of the Store. So ideally there should some pleasant boys and girls in the Store uniforms, welcoming customers to the Store. A visit to the Store should be an exhilarating experience. Bright and smiling greeters lure customers.

103. Help Desk:

It is important to have a Help Desk, if the Store is large (say, having more than eight to 10 checkouts), where customers can have their queries answered.

104. Loyalty schemes:

Loyalty programmes allure customers to the Store for repeat visits. The management should develop a loyalty programme even before the launch. It should be well publicised so that customers know about it. The Store software should incorporate the loyalty programme.

105. Loyalty cards:

Customers should be issued 'Loyalty Cards' with their details imprinted on them. Loyalty Cards should be required to be shown or even swiped at the cash counters, when customers shop.

106. Policy on customer returns - Product, time, and usage:

The Store policy on product returns, i.e. which products can be returned, or exchanged, within specified timings and at what stage of usage, etc., should be detailed by the management. This policy should be clearly stated on the invoices, website, etc. of the Store, so that customers know. This will avoid misunderstandings and customer complaints at a later date.

107. Suggestion box and slips:

Cards inviting customer feedback and suggestions should be placed prominently at the checkout counters. Customers should be encouraged to provide their e-mails or telephone numbers or addresses. Cards filled by the customers should be stored carefully and sent on a daily or a weekly basis to be customer services management. Every meaningful complaint should be acknowledged and appropriate action initiated. Moreover, feedback should be provided to the customer.

108. Goods returns area:

There should be an exclusive section or counter where customers can return or exchange their goods. It is best to have a separate area for this, to avoid inconvenience to customers who are making regular purchases.

109. Polite service - Complaints:

Customers in most parts of the world are very concerned about the type of service they will receive, when they visit an outlet with a quality complaint or if they wish to return a defective product. When a salesman and a store sell a product they earn a commission and revenues, respectively. However, when a product is returned due to some defect, they lose revenue. A customer unhappy with the service on a complaint will be lost forever. However, a customer, whose complaint is attended to expeditiously and politely, will be a friend of the outlet for life. The staff at the complaints counter should be very polite and helpful and do their best to accommodate the customer.

110. Helpers at exits:

A few helpers at the exit can help senior citizens, the old and the infirm to get their packages to their cars, cabs etc.

111. Newsletter for consumers:

If the Store is large and has many locations, it will make marketing sense to issue a monthly newsletter to the customers, via e-mail. The newsletter could provide details on new offerings, promotions, new locations, etc.

112. Periodic catalogues on products, benefits, prices etc.

Issuing periodic catalogues detailing special offer and promotions also boosts sales. Many electronic stores and supermarkets issue a monthly catalogue listing the special offers for the month. The general practice is to issue printed copies at the entrance of the Store. However, mailing these catalogues by e-mail to the customers will yield better results. The frequency of promotional e-mails to the customers must not be too often to avoid them from becoming spam.

113. "May I help you" badges, staff and management:

The Store should generate a friendly and warm experience. Hence all badges of the staff and management should have an offer to help, imprinted on it, e.g. "May I please help you?" The staff should be trained to be friendly with the customers, but not get familiar.

114. Directory of customers - Contact details, likes and dislikes, etc.:

The Store should prepare a directory of regular customers who have enrolled in the loyalty programme. The IT software will record the cumulative purchases of the customer on a continuous basis. However, the sales staff should record any special preferences or nuances of the customer. For instance, if the customer is a senior citizen and needs a wheel chair it should be noted on his page. Again if a customer is always buying white formal shirts, it should be noted. These customer notes will help the Store to enhance service to the customer.

115. Home Delivery policy - Bulk orders:

The Store should have a clear policy on home delivery of products, if they exceed a certain financial limit. The limit will depend on the type of outlet and the products being sold. Electronic and furniture items have to be delivered at home. Many grocery supermarkets in India and abroad have also started delivering large grocery orders at the homes of their customers.

116. Orders for parties and offices - Bulk:

The Store can also seek bulk orders for parties at home or office or the monthly requirements (say, groceries) of office teams and deliver the same. This will also boost sales.

117. Shopping bags retention area:

The Store management will have to provide an area at the entrance where shoppers can leave their shopping bags from other outlets, which cannot be permitted into the premises. This is an essential facility in a large outlet to prevent loss or pilferage.

118. Games for children:

In large destination stores like hypermarkets for groceries, furniture, electronics, etc. the children get jaded when their parents shop. The parents are unable to shop with concentration since they have to manage their children too. It is worthwhile to have play areas, where the children can play and refresh themselves, whilst their parents shop unperturbed.

119. Attractions and gifts for children:

Children have a foremost impact on the outlet that will be visited, through their parents. If a child enjoys being in an outlet due to the ambience, friendliness, play area, etc., the chances of repeat visits are augmented. So it is a good idea to have small gifts for children who visit the Store. McDonald's have built armies of loyal kids' customers across the world by having special kid menus, gifts, toys in their 'Happy Meals', etc.

L. Information Technology:

120. System to be used:

Information Technology (IT) is the nerve centre of a Modern Retail business. Modern retail runs on IT. If IT does not run even for a day, the Store has to shut for that day. So the selection of the IT systems is a crucial decision.

The IT company or vendor should be able to service the Store on an on-going basis later. It is thus important to study the best retail IT systems options available in the market before making a decision. Presentations and quotations should be invited from the top five to ten IT service providers, prior to selecting a vendor.

121. Standard Operating Procedures:

Standard Operating Procedures should be written for every section and activity of the Store e.g. purchase, inventory management, sales, billing, merchandising, sales returns, promotions, staff matters, reports, MIS, etc.

These should be discussed amongst the operating managers prior to finalisation. Writing the Manual of Operations sufficiently in advance of the Store opening is useful, since the processes and procedures contribute to formulating the standard operating procedures.

122. Processes, Point of sale (POS), support systems:

Store management should undertake a detailed review to ensure that the systems will blend well with various organisational and Store processes, point of sales, inventory management, support systems, etc.

123. Vendor ratings and perceptions:

It is useful to undertake a detailed review of the various IT vendors who submit proposals. The vendors are generally prepared to give references of their clients. Meeting some of the clients of the vendors is essential and will give a fair picture of their capabilities.

124. Installation and execution:

The responsibility for installation and execution of the new IT systems in the Store should be that of the vendor. Even if there is a dedicated IT team in the Store, the responsibility for execution of the new Store IT systems should be with the IT vendor. The vendor should also have the responsibility for training the staff.

125. Testing of equipment and trial runs:

The new IT systems should be installed and ready to deliver at least six to eight weeks before the Store opens for business. The lead-time will provide the opportunity to train the staff and also check that all the processes are working as planned. Moreover, the purchases and inventories have to be entered into the system before the opening day. Inventories may arrive three to four weeks, before the Store commences operations.

126. Corporate website:

The Store must also create a corporate website providing the Company profile, Company Values, Management Team, Store locations, Customer Care contact details, etc. The product catalogues can also be provided on the website and online purchase of products and services can also be facilitated, for the customers. The website must be user friendly and updated regularly.

M. Key Management Information Systems (MIS) Reports:

Some of the important reports that need to be generated regularly are:

127. Daily, weekly sales:

These reports are for the operating managers and the general management team. The management team should be able to see the sales on a daily and weekly basis. The reports should be by item, categories and groups of products, so that it is possible to review the performance of each product or section in the Store.

Moreover, if the managers want to drill deeper to identify the specific sales of some product, brand or model, the reporting system should have the flexibility to provide the same. For instance, in a store selling cameras and mobiles telephones if the management needs to identify the five top selling models, the system should generate the information instantaneously.

128. Monthly reports:

The monthly reports should provide details of sales by product, category, brand, etc., to enable operating managers to take decisions based on hard data. The monthly report should also provide data by store, in case of multiple stores.

129. Sales contribution, 20:80:

The 20 per cent of the products, which contributes 80 per cent of the sales, should be reviewed on a daily basis. This will help to focus sales attention and promotions on those products, which generate high revenues and profits.

130. Inventory levels:

Inventory levels should be reviewed on a weekly basis to ensure that no fast selling products are ever out of stock. The inventories of fast selling items like mobile phones in an electronics store need to be reviewed on a daily basis, to ensure continuous availability of stocks.

131. Payables:

Payables should also be monitored on a weekly and monthly basis to ensure that the bills of vendors are being cleared expeditiously. Vendors respect companies that clear their dues on schedule without reminders.

132. Monthly Profit and Loss, Balance Sheets:

Smart CEOs and promoters will not wait till a quarter or a full year to know how the business is performing. They will want to get monthly Profit and Loss Statements and Balance Sheets so that they can initiate course correction manoeuvres very early.

133. Weekly Cash Flow Statements:

A weekly review of the Cash Flow Statements will also reveal the cash health of the Store.

134. Profitability by category, brand, franchisor and vendor:

It is imperative to analyse profitability statements in rigorous detail. Profitability statements should be reviewed by category, brand and even franchisor or vendor. The operations team should identify laggards, which are not contributing to profits and formulate time bound turnaround plans for them.

135. Ages of inventories:

This statement highlights items, which do not sell well. They pile up in the warehouse of the Store, occupying space and blocking working capital. It is useful to clear slow selling stocks every quarter to free space and money.

N.   General Operations:

136. Manual of Operations and Business Process:

Professional retailers run their business through systems and procedures. The management must ensure that all the operations of the Store are thus written in a Standard Operations Manual. Operation manuals should be written early three to six months prior to the Store commencing, to reduce any ambiguity at a later stage. The Manual should be comprehensive and detailed. It should prescribe the operating procedures for all activities in the Store. It will be like a 'bible' for the Store staff, in which all processes and procedures are clarified.

137. Monthly Operations Review Meeting:

A monthly Operations Review Meeting (ORM) should be held, say on the second Monday of each month, to review the sales and financial performance of the previous month and fine-tune the goals for the current month. The CEO should chair it. At this meeting the performance of various products, profitability, consumer promotions, inventory levels and staff members should be discussed. All Store managers and departmental heads should attend the meeting.

138. Profitability of the Store:

Every effort should be made to make the Store profitable from the first year onwards. So there will be need for constant control of overheads and frugality. Retailing is a tough and competitive business.

If the Store does well, the promoters and management may consider expanding and opening additional Stores in other malls or towns. Nevertheless, the expansion should be guided by the principle that each Store should stand on its own feet and churn a profit. If some Stores are not delivering profits, management should develop a time bound turnaround plan to make them financially viable.

139. Competition or market prices:

It is important to monitor competition prices for the same or similar products in other outlets. If most outlets are selling a formal suit for USD 300 and if the Store price for a similar suit is USD 500, then some price correction is essential. Any sharp variances in prices between the Store products and those of the competition should also be discussed at the Monthly Operations Meetings.

140. Researching the market:

The CEO, senior management and the buyers should ceaselessly study the market on a regional and global basis, for the products that they sell. Consumer trends in fashion, food products and electronics are constantly changing. The world is becoming younger by the day. It is important to study the behaviour and consumption habits of younger generations, to be able to serve them in all product areas.

The Store management should always be a few steps ahead of the market in analysing economic, sociological and buyer behaviour trends.

141. Fixed prices:

Most Modern Retail stores have fixed prices. However, some stores have the practice of giving the sales staff or supervisor some flexibility to reduce one or two per cent prices on items like electronics or furniture. This practice is best avoided and is best to adhere to a policy of fixed prices in the Store.

142. Critical role of buyers:

The quality of merchandise being sold in the Stores, results in the sale. The buyers who purchase the merchandise for the Store have a critical role in the success of the Store. The Store can only sell the merchandise placed in it, which is purchased by the buyers. So if the buyers have not read or understood the market thoroughly, they will buy merchandise, which will not move from the shelves.

Thus, the buyers of the Stores should be top class professionals who are abreast of market trends. For instance, a buyer for an apparel Store should know the latest trends in fashion and fabrics. A buyer for an electronics Store should update himself on latest technologies, models and launches.

143. Walk the floors:

Senior management of the Store should spend at least half a day every week on the shop floors talking to staff members and observing customers. It is very useful to get feedback and ideas from the shop floors. Many managers do not realise the importance of spending time on the shop floors. The shop floors are the best schools to learn retailing

144. Timeliness in innovation and logistics:

Large fashion retailers pride themselves in identifying a new fashion trend, producing the new apparel and disseminating the new merchandise to thousands of retail outlets across the globe, in a time span of weeks. So it becomes vital to be sharp in spotting market changes, incorporating them in product designs and placing the stocks expeditiously on the shop floors through excellent logistics.

145. Customer complaints and Suggestions Statement:

Customer feedback in the form of complaints and suggestions are an enormous source of feedback on the Store. Every customer complaint should be acknowledged and the customer should be informed of the corrective action taken on the issue raised by him or her. Customers spend their time writing down complaints or suggestions and they are entitled to get an acknowledgement and feedback.

The monthly list of customer complaints and suggestions should be discussed at the monthly Operation Review Meeting or the Monthly Board Meeting.

146. Price tags to underscore branding:

The price tags attached to the merchandise should also be used to underscore the logo, name and promise of the Store.

O. Retail is people:

147. Organisation chart:

A fundamental rule of building a new team for any business is to develop an organisation chart, which shows the people required at various levels, for all the functions. The organisation chart is based on the various activities to be undertaken in the Store and the quality and levels of people required. It also helps to determine the annual salary bill of the store.

148. Number of staff:

The number of staff required in the Store should be estimated by function and level, i.e. sales staff, merchandisers, security staff, visualisers, floor managers, category managers, accounts staff, cashiers, etc.

149. Budgeting for floor staff:

It is provident to recruit 10 to 15 per cent extra floor sales staff to have some cover for exigencies. During festival periods some stores have extra working hours necessitating additional staff. Moreover, there is some natural attrition and turnover of the staff, which should be provided for.

150. Job descriptions and specifications:

The job descriptions of all the assignments in the Store along with the job specifications, which delineate the qualifications, skills and experience required for executing an assignment, should be prepared. This exercise helps to identify the most appropriate candidates and reduces the level of subjectivity in the selection process.

151. Gender in recruitment:

Almost all stores employ men and women for all departments. However, in certain types of stores, a few sensitivities are obligatory. For instance, in an apparel store, it is best to recruit girls for the lingerie sections. Women customer would find it more comfortable.

152. Countries of origin:

If the Store is being built in country, which has ample local staff available, then there is no need to determine the countries from where the staff will be recruited. Thus, if the Store is in India, China, Brazil or Kenya, there is adequate local talent and staff available.

However, if the Store is in a Middle East country like the UAE, Bahrain, Qatar, etc., it may be necessary to recruit from other countries like India, Egypt, Sri Lanka, etc. depending on the type of positions being filled. For instance, if the recruitment is for an apparel outlet for Arabs, then it may be necessary to recruit staff from Egypt or Syria, which offers Arab-speaking staff.

153. Formulation of relevant tests:

To improve the objectivity in recruitments, it is best to have some vocabulary, numerical and skill proficiency tests, through which it will be possible to identify the most suitable candidates. An external HR agency can assist in conducting these tests, if there are a large number of candidates to be interviewed.

154. Formation of recruitment team:

The recruitment of staff can be done by the Store management or outsourced to an external agency. It is best to recruit by forming a small internal recruitment cell in the initial stages comprising of Store managers and perhaps a Human Relations advisor who can help to identify and source candidates.

155. Schedule of recruitment:

There should be a clear schedule of recruitment, so that all the positions are filled some weeks prior to the Store opening. Fresh recruits have to be trained and groomed before they take charge of the reins. Hence it is provident for the team to be in place sufficiently in advance.

156. Administrative arrangements:

The administrative arrangements for the new recruits should be in place before they join. Their medical tests and appointment letters should be organised expeditiously. It is useful to put all new staff though a medical exam through a hospital, before issuing the appointment letter.

157. Arrival and housing arrangements:

If some of the staff is coming from abroad they should be received at the airport through some agency so that they enter the country smoothly. If they are to be provided housing on joining, the facilities should be ready when they arrive.

158. Transport arrangements:

If the staff stays far away from the Store, it would make sense to arrange a bus to pick them up daily and drop them to their homes. In UAE since most of the sales staff comprises of expatriates and are hence often provided housing and transport by the store management.

P. **Staff and Service:**

159. Grooming:

Grooming and self-presentation need enormous attention in any store. The staff should be counselled to pay attention to details, i.e. combing of hair, regular haircuts, clean finger nails, attention to body odour, etc. These details are important, because their neglect can infuriate customers and can cost a sale.

160. Uniforms of staff:

The uniforms should be finalised based on the concept, the ambience of the Store and the type of products being stored. The uniforms of the staff should be decided in advance. Most retail stores have dispensed with a tie as part of the uniform.

Uniforms should have a pleasant colour and should be easy to maintain.

The Store management can take a view whether they would like the managers of the Store also to be dressed in the same uniform as the staff.

161. Frequency of washing:

Uniforms should be changed daily. A set of clothes should never be used for two days consequently. Sometimes the stores are not air-conditioned and perspiration marks on the clothes look unhygienic and can peeve the customers.

162. Treatment of women and girls:

Most retail stores employ a large number of young boys and girls. Since they work long hours together on the floors, they often become very friendly. However, staff should be counselled not to get over-familiar. A stray comment made by someone could lead to a disciplinary issue. Hence the Store should have a clear and well-known policy on the respectful, fair and equal treatment of lady employees.

163. Language skills:

The Store staff should be able to speak the local language, in addition to the main language being used in the geographical area. For instance, in a store in Mumbai, the sales staff should be fluent in English, Hindi and Marathi. In Dubai some sales staff should know English and Arabic. In Brazil, it would help if the sales staff also knew some English, in addition to Portuguese.

164. Drinking water and beverages:

It is important to ensure that the staff has adequate arrangements for drinking water and beverages like tea, coffee, cold drinks, etc., in the recreation rooms.

165. Shoeshine arrangements:

Staff members should be encouraged to ensure that their shoes are shining at all times. They should clean their shoes before coming to work. However, shoe brushes and polishes should be kept in the staff room for an emergency.

166. Best word - Smile:

All staff should be encouraged to smile, all the time. A smile can dissolve many customer grievances and grouses. A smile can enliven a store, more than any powerful electrical light.

167. First aid boxes:

A well-equipped first aid box should be maintained in the recreation room, to cater to minor injuries, bruises, etc.

168. Refrigerator and microwave:

Some of the staff members may be fetching snacks from their homes for their respites. There should be a refrigerator and a microwave, so that they can store their food hygienically and then heat it before eating.

169. Daily morning meetings:

The Store Manager should hold a daily morning meeting of all the staff. At this meeting the sales performance of the previous day should be analysed. The meeting should also be used for determining the priorities and targets for the day.

170. Operating floor rules and disciplinary situations:

The Store manager should also use these morning meetings to clarify the operating rules on the floors. For instance, some outlets have a policy of not permitting their sales staff to use mobile telephone on the sales floors.

171. Customer management skills:

The Staff should also be trained to manage the customers who visit the Store. Customers can be moody, unpredictable and demanding. Sometimes customers are not very clear about the exact size, features or model of a product that they need to buy, e.g. a new television. The sales staff should help the customer to decide what he needs to buy. Sometimes customers can take hours to decide the sizes of the clothes that fit them. Sales staff have to have infinite patience.

172. Training and development:

The Store staff should be exposed to regular training and development programmes, conducted in-house or through external consultants. The modules should cover product knowledge, grooming and communication skills.

173. Theft, pilferage, shrinkages issues and responsibilities:

The Store should have lucid policies on any thefts, pilferages and shrinkages. These should be reported to the management immediately.

174. Lockers for staff:

Members of the staff should have lockers for keeping their clothes and valuables when they are at work. Items should not be left in the lockers, after the shift is over. Lockers should be rotated between the staff members.

175. Staff meal timings:

The staff timings for meals, refreshments, etc. should be specified for their convenience. The recesses should be staggered so that there are always adequate numbers of staff on the sales floors.

176. Staff eating areas:

There should be adequate space for a cafeteria for the staff to have their meals and refreshments.

177. Staff recreation area and room:

If the Store is large in size (i.e. over 10,000 square feet), there should also be a recreation room for the staff where they can relax.

178. Staff discounts permitted:

The discounts that are permitted to the staff on the purchases from the Store should be cleared by senior management and explained clearly. There should also be an annual limit on staff purchases with discounts. The annual limit is necessary to ensure that staff members use the discount for their own purchases and not for their friends.

179. Quiet room:

It is a great idea to have a Quiet room with a bed if space permits, for female staff members to rest, should they need to.

Q. Targets and Incentives:

180. Monthly and quarterly targets:

The annual target for each section of the Store should be split into quarterly and monthly targets, to ensure improved accountability.

181. System of incentives:

The targets should be linked to the incentives to the staff. About 70 to 75 per cent of the monthly salary should be fixed for sales personnel. The balance salary of 25 to 30 per cent should be linked to the monthly sales targets achievement.

182. Communication of targets and incentives:

The sales targets and their interlinking with the incentives should be clearly explained to the staff, so that there is no misunderstanding at any stage.

183. Transparency in incentives:

It is also important to be transparent in the calculations of the incentives, to ensure staff satisfaction and confidence.

184. Weekly review of targets:

Concerned category managers should review target achievement on a weekly basis. Sharp managers tend to set daily targets for their team members.

185. Responsibility for administration:

The responsibility for recording achievements against targets and calculating the incentives should be with the Human Relations department. They should also keep all the records.

R. **Training and Development:**

186. Areas of Training:

On joining the Store all new employees, irrespective of level, should have to undergo an Induction Programme for two to three days, wherein they are briefed about the promoters, the Store philosophy and the business of the group. This should be mandatory to ensure that all new recruits are aware about the group and its values.

187. Focus - Customer service and technical knowledge:

There should also be separate training sessions in sales, customer service for recruits who will be at the sales counters dealing with customers. The courses will seek to strengthen sales skills, customer management and the ability to handle sales objections. To provide some technical expertise to the sales staff they should also be exposed to some basic knowledge about the technical aspects of the products. Role-playing sessions should also be organised.

188. Number of participants:

The Induction Course should ideally be restricted to a maximum of 30 to 40 participants. The Customer service and Technical sessions should be restricted to about 25 to 30 participants. Both these programmes should be two to three day segments and be intensive in rigour.

189. Survey of external agencies:

It is worthwhile to survey of external agencies or resources available for the training programmes. Internal resources may be rather limited in the initial stages and they may be tight for time. Ideally the faculty should comprise of internal and external resources.

190. Selection of agency:

In selecting an external agency, it is important to ensure that they have some experience in training retail professionals. The agency should have some staff with practical retail experience.

191. Involve suppliers for technical inputs:

If the Store is selling some electronic or technical product like computers, mobile phones, etc., it is useful to involve the suppliers in the training programmes. They could provide technical knowledge to the staff. Supplier companies are generally delighted to support the teams of their customers, in the area of skill enhancement.

192. Feedback from participants:

After the training programmes are complete, the participants should be required to fill a feedback form on the overall programme and the on specific sessions and individual speakers. The feedback will help to improve the quality of future sessions.

S. Cash Collections:

193. Policy cash, credit and cheques:

The policy of the Store about the acceptable modes of payment should be clearly displayed at the cash counters.

194. Responsibility for cash:

The responsibility for cash accounting should be clearly ascribed. Cash should also be covered by insurance.

195. Daily cash collections - Reconciliation:

All cash, cheques, etc. should be reconciled after every shift before a new cashier takes over.

196. Overnight safe keeping:

If the cash has to be kept overnight at the Store, there should be adequate security arrangements for storing it. Management should determine the persons responsible for overnight safe cash keeping.

197. Shortages reporting issues:

Any shortages of cash should be reported immediately to the management.

198. Cash memo records:

All copies of bills, cash memos and credit card records should be fastidiously maintained in the office records, to facilitate retrievals if required in the future.

199. Deposits in banks etc./frequency/responsibility

The modus operandi, frequency and responsibility of depositing cash and cheques in the banks should be clearly specified and also manualised.

200. Insurance

The Store should have all insurance policies in place, pertaining to inventories, pilferages, cash, equipment, etc.

T. Security in Store:

201. Number of entrances and exits in Store:

The number of entrances and exits in the Store should be minimised to manage customer traffic and the inventories.

202. Number of guards required and positioning:

The number of security guards required in the Store, should be determined in consultation with the security company. It is useful to have some female security guards also. Moreover, security guards can also be dressed up in the Store uniforms and double as greeters.

203. Number of cameras:

The number of CCTV cameras and their location should be finalised in consultation with the security company and the mall management.

204. Room for CCTV monitors:

There should be a separate room to accommodate all the CCTV screens.

205. Room for guards:

Provision should also be made for a room or a space for the guards, for changing into uniforms, etc.

206. Connection to monitors in office:

The CCTV cameras should also be connected to the regional offices, so that concerned managers can oversee any part of the Store at any time.

U.   Equipment Maintenance:

207. List of equipment with details and dates:

All the equipment in the Store i.e. counters, trolleys, furniture, etc. should be listed and inventoried.

208. Maintenance frequency, schedule and records:

There should be maintenance schedule for equipment that requires to be serviced at periodic intervals, e.g. air-conditioners, generators, trolley wheels, etc.

209. Painting maintenance:

The Store should be well painted at all times. Shoddy or patchy walls create a damaging impression of the Store. It is useful to have a painting contractor who will undertake regular touch-ups, at short notice as and when required.

210. Replacements and repairs budgets, and responsibilities:

There should be a maintenance and repairs budget for the Store. It is also very important to have an excellent contractor to undertake repairs on a timely basis. Repairs in the Store should be undertaken on an emergency basis (within 12 to 24 hours) to preserve the image and ambience of the Store. For instance, if a tile breaks or becomes loose, it should be repaired in the night.

V. Warehouses and Backrooms:

211. Purpose of warehouses:

The Store will need some warehouses or backrooms to store extra inventories of various products. These should be located in the same neighbourhood as the Store, so that replenishment of inventories can be swift.

212. Requirements of space based on lead delivery periods, etc.:

The amount of warehouse space required will depend on the size of the Store and the levels of inventories required to be stored. If all the inventories are imported and have a long lead-time for deliveries, higher levels of stocks may have to be maintained in the warehouse.

213. Visibility:

Warehouses should be so designed that the stacked stocks should always be visible, so that retrievals should be easy.

214. Flooring to handle movement of trolleys, etc.:

The flooring of the warehouse should be smooth, so that trolleys can be moved easily.

215. Fitments and racks:

Since the fitments and racks are often imported it is useful to maintain some extra inventories of these items also for urgent replacements or additions.

216. Trolleys:

There should be adequate trolleys in the Store so that customers do not have to hunt for them. Trolleys should also be maintained in working condition and damaged ones should be removed immediately from the floors and refurbished.

217. Locks – Keys and responsibilities:

The responsibility for locking the Store every night and the holding of the keys, should be clearly specified.

218. Loading and unloading bays:

There should be adequate number of loading and unloading bays, with the prescribed heights so that containers can be unloaded conveniently.

219. Cleanliness and orderliness:

There should be high levels of cleanliness and orderliness in the warehouse to protect the inventories from dust, pollution, insects, etc. irrespective of the type of products. The warehouses should be as well maintained as the Store.

W. Restrooms:

220. Restrooms Management:

There should be separate restrooms for the visiting customers and the staff.

Restrooms should be kept clean at all times. This gives the clear message to the staff about the importance of hygiene and cleanliness. Sometimes the toilets of the customers and managers are well maintained, but those of the staff are neglected. This is unfair. A CEO I know, would often use the staff toilets just to check on the cleanliness levels.

221. Separate facilities for men and women:

There should be separate toilets for men and women. This is also a legal requirement in many countries.

222. Cleaning schedule:

Restrooms should be cleaned at regular intervals. Ideally a cleaner should be stationed there throughout the day, for regular cleaning.

223. Cleaning materials:

The cleaning materials used to maintain the toilets should be specified and should always be available.

224. Ventilation arrangements:

Toilets should be well ventilated, unless they are air-conditioned.

225. Hand drying machines and disposable tissues:

There should be arrangements for hand drying machines or adequate disposable tissues in the toilets.

226. Space for advertising:

The toilet entrance area provides some spaces for advertising. These spaces should be used for advertising and to generate some revenues.

X. Launch of Store:

227. Finalisation of advertising agency:

It is important to have an able and established advertising agency handling all communications. The agency should be finalised at least six to nine months prior to the launch so that it has adequate time to prepare all the concepts, present them to the management and then execute them.

228. Finalisation of Events management agency:

It would also be provident to appoint an Events management agency to manage all the launch activities.

229. Media launch i.e. press, television radio, etc.:

The advertising agency can advise on which media to deploy for launch i.e. press, television or radio, depending on the size of the Store and the budgets.

Whilst press is widely used and radio too occasionally, television is normally not used for launching retail stores, due to the cost factor. However, if the Store is a huge concept, television should also be considered. For instance, if Ikea or Carrefour launches their stores in a new country, they should definitely consider using television.

230. Outdoor media:

Outdoor media like hoardings, bus shelters, bus panels, etc. are very effective in generating rapid awareness. These should also be considered depending on the budgets for the launch programme.

231. Objectives of the launch:

The objectives of the Store launch should be clear. Is the goal to get many customers visiting the Store on the very first day? Then offer a promotion or discount for the first three days. Is the goal to achieve widespread awareness of the Store in the initial days? Then, advertise heavily.

232. Campaign periods:

The time span during which the launch advertising campaign should run should be determined in advance. Ideally the launch campaign should last for about six months.

233. List of activities:

Some of the activities that can be conducted on the launch day are: special discounts, posters, banners, etc. in the mall, inviting a celebrity, newspapers advertisements or insertions, press and television coverage, refreshments, gifts for children, etc.

234. Budgets:

All the launch activities of the Store should be listed, costed and a budget prepared.

235. Date of launch:

The date of launching the Store should not clash with any other major event, to ensure that potential customers are not diverted. For instance, if the launch is in Mumbai and there is a major cricket match, it would be best to scan for an alternate day to ensure maximum customer visits.

236. Co-ordinate with mall management:

If the Store is in a mall, some of the launch activities may involve liaising with the mall management, to avoid any inconvenience to other stores.

237. Invites:

The invitations for the launch programme should be sent at least a fortnight before the date of launch, so that guests can plan their visits sufficiently in advance.

238. Celebrity inauguration:

Some outlets invite a movie star or leading sports personalities to cut the ribbon and inaugurate the Store. This has some advantages. Movie stars and sports personalities attract visitors and media coverage. However, this may not necessarily result in sales.

239. Launch function:

The actual launch function should ideally be organised within the Store itself so that the visitors have an opportunity to review the merchandise and make some purchases.

240. Briefing of staff:

The entire staff of the Store should be briefed on all the launch activities. This will enthuse them. They will also feel involved.

241. Greeters:

There should be special greeters at the entrance of the Store on the date of the launch. The senior management of the company or the Store should also be present to greet and receive the guests and customers on the first day.

242. Press conference:

A press conference should be kept at least two days prior to the launch date to ensure that news of the Store launch is widely published in the local newspapers.

243. Refreshments for customers and staff:

There should be some refreshments for the special guests and the staff after the launch event. The launch event may extend from two to four hours and guests should not be kept thirsty or hungry.

244. Incentives, free gifts to consumers and staff:

There should be some gift or memento for the guests and the staff to mark the day of the launch of the Store.

245. Gifts, balloons for kids, etc.:

Small toys and balloons will keep the children happy and occupied on the day of the launch.

246. Show for kids: face painting, painting, etc.:

To enthuse the children who are visiting the Store, a few additional activities like face painting, games, painting contests, etc., could be organised.

247. Anticipate and factor competition reactions:

The competition is bound to react if the launch programme is successful and lures customers. So it is necessary to be prepared for an additional set of promotional activities to be initiated, in response to competition reactions.

248. Repeat advertising:

It will be necessary to continue repeat advertising and promotions after the launch phase also, though at a lower frequency.

249. Payments to all vendors:

Payments to all the vendors who have enabled the launch of the Store should be made as per terms. This is important to build a good image in the market for a new Store. Vendors should love to do business with the new Store. Timely payments will help.

250. Thanks mails:

After the launch of the Store appropriate letters of thanks should be sent to all agencies and persons who have contributed to it, e.g. advertising and event agencies, mall management, press, etc.

251. Calibrating results:

The milestones that are set for the launch should be specified and calibrated. For instance, if the goal is to get 15,000 visitors to the Store on the first day, then the number of visitors to the Store on the day should be counted and compared to the target.

Y. Marketing and Promotion - Post launch:

252. Marketing and promotions:

Marketing and promotions should continue even during the post launch phase. An annual calendar of activities and events should be drawn at the commencement of each year. The annual marketing plan will cover the promotions and offers each month for various categories of products, monthly visuals and displays plan, media plans, publicity activities, etc. for the full year. All these activities should be set for every quarter and month so that the brand managers and category managers are fully geared for the marketing initiatives.

253. Vendor participation:

The marketing team should involve the vendors in the annual marketing plans and activities. The vendors should also be requested to offer special promotions to the customers through the Store. In the Middle East vendors participate actively in Store promotions by contributing discounts, consumer offers and publicity material.

254. Festival offers:

Across the world festivals are times for massive shopping sprees. Christmas in the USA and Europe, 'Diwali' in India and the 'Eid' festival in the Middle East are all occasions for customers to shop for themselves and also buy gifts for others. So during festival periods, the stores should don a festive look with appropriate visuals and merchandising, and have a host of offers to rivet the attention of the customers.

Z. Strategic E-commerce Initiatives:

255. Online sales, etc.:

Online sales through e-commerce are augmenting across the world. Hence, the management of the Store must decide whether they would like to make their products available online also, through their own website or through other established online retailers like Amazon.

256. Social media or digital marketing:

The Store management should actively consider entering the e-commerce space. This will necessitate engaging in digital marketing via social media. Social media will enable the business to interact with its customers. The posts and messages on Social Media platforms such as Twitter, Facebook, Instagram, LinkedIn, Snapchat, etc. provide insights into consumer needs and also provide feedback. Depending on the size of the Store, either appropriate persons can be recruited or the work can be farmed out to an external agency.

257. Take Your Breath away:

An outstanding Store can take from six to twelve months to become a reality from the idea stage to a physical form. Throughout the endeavour, the retailer must aim to create a Store, that will "take the customer's breath away", when he visits the outlet. The customer should say, as in the song in the Tom Cruise movie 'Top Gun":

'Take my breath away
Take my breath away'

258. Rejoice:

Building a new concept store is a labour of love. So, rejoice when it is ready.

14

READY RECKONER: 'NUTS AND BOLTS'

(D: Discussed; F: Finalised; E: Executed)

Activity		D	F	E
A.	**Developing The Concept:**			
1.	Value Proposition			
2.	Market segmentation			
3.	Theme of the store			
4.	Ambience			
5.	Destination store or "me too"			
6.	Category killer			
7.	Budget for Store			
8.	Meeting with CEOs			
B.	**Agreements and Understandings:**			
9.	Board members, on board			
10.	Permissions and meetings - government, local authorities			
11.	Terms and Conditions			
12.	Rentals of property			
13.	Basis of rentals, flat rent, or per cent of sales			
14.	Number of years' agreement			
15.	Possibilities of renewal/extension			
16.	Refining the Agreements			
17.	Franchisers- Policies on returns, display support, etc.			
18.	Franchisers- Training and Development			

Activity			D	F	E
	19.	Signing of Agreements, Disputes			
C.	**Location:**				
	20.	Mall or High Street?			
	21.	Floor of the Mall			
	22.	Neighbouring outlets			
	23.	Proximity to entrance/restaurants/movie theatres			
D.	**Constructing the Store:**				
	24.	Finalise Architect			
	25.	Drawings			
	26.	Construction Contractor			
	27.	Scope of work			
	28.	Penalty Clauses			
	29.	Range of materials and specifications			
	30.	Introduction fees – architects			
	31.	Segmentation of the store by product category			
	32.	Any shop-in- shop possibilities			
	33.	Locating various categories			
	34.	Space for advertising			
	35.	Space for promotions and merchandisers			
	36.	Number of cash tills			
	37.	Planning and installing Public Address System			
	38.	Music in Store			
E.	**Selection of Floors, Ceiling, Lights:**				
	39.	Tiles and Lights: Designs and patterns			
	40.	Use of interior, external lights			
	41.	Intensity of lights			
	42.	Colours of lights			

	Activity	D	F	E
43.	Imported or locally available			
44.	Price and quality comparisons			
45.	Lead times			
46.	Selection of vendors			
47.	Determining prices/terms/penalty clauses			
F.	**Fitments:**			
48.	Types and range desired			
49.	Quantities and Numbers			
50.	Local or imported			
51.	Manufacturing material			
52.	Colours			
53.	Pricing			
54.	Lead period for delivery			
G.	**Merchandising the store:**			
55.	List of merchandise			
56.	List of suppliers			
57.	Agreements with vendors			
58.	Lead times			
59.	Date expiry stocks – timings of supply			
60.	Placement of stocks on shelves, replenishments, etc.			
61.	Inventory management in Store and warehouse			
62.	Monthly, quarterly stock audits			
63.	Payment period			
64.	Returns policy			
H.	**Branding and Signages:**			
65.	Name of the Store			
66.	High visibility spots for Store name			
67.	Approved designs, formats, scripts			

Activity	D	F	E
68. Approved logos			
69. Colours			
70. Registration of names, logos			
71. High visibility areas and lighting			
72. Check local languages translations			
73. Visiting card formats and branding			
74. Deploy invoice to underscore branding and logo			
I. Visuals in Store:			
75. Concepts			
76. Location spots			
77. Exact sizes of windows, displays			
78. Renting of windows, visual spaces to maximise revenue			
79. Content of Visuals: Product, display and materials			
80. Changing visuals			
81. Breaking monotony			
82. Use of flowers			
83. Internal or external management			
J. Displays and Merchandising:			
84. Areas of displays, merchandising			
85. Responsibilities for merchandising, displays			
86. Maintenance, cleaning of show cases			
87. Policy on posters			
88. Frames for posters, announcers			
89. Discussions with vendors for participation in displays etc.			
90. Charges/fees for space and promotions in store			

Activity	D	F	E
91. Rotation of displays.			
92. Placement of screens			
93. Carry bags of products: material, colours, printed matter			
94. Product catalogues			
K. Customer Service:			
95. Corporate statement			
96. Space for corporate statement			
97. Welcome – signage			
98. Thanks – signage			
99. Store locator			
100. Category locator			
101. Advisors/Product Consultants			
102. Greeters at entrances			
103. Help Desk			
104. Loyalty scheme			
105. Loyalty cards			
106. Policy on customer returns: product, time, and usage			
107. Suggestion box, slips			
108. Goods returns area			
109. Polite service: complaints			
110. Helpers at exits			
111. Newsletter for consumers			
112. Periodic catalogues on products, benefits, prices etc.			
113. "May I help you" badges, staff and management			
114. Directory of customers: contact details, likes/dislikes etc.			
115. Home Delivery policy: bulk orders			

Activity		D	F	E
116.	Orders for parties, offices: bulk			
117.	Shopping bags retention area			
118.	Games for children			
119.	Attractions/gifts for children			
L.	**Information Technology:**			
120.	System to be used			
121.	Standard Operating Procedures			
122.	Processes, POS, support systems			
123.	Vendor ratings and perceptions			
124.	Installation and execution			
125.	Testing of equipment and trial runs			
126.	Corporate Website			
M.	**Key MIS Reports:**			
127.	Daily, weekly sales			
128.	Monthly reports			
129.	Sales contribution 20:80			
130.	Inventory levels			
131.	Payables			
132.	Monthly Profit & Loss, Balance Sheets			
133.	Profitability by category, brand, franchisor, vendor			
134.	Weekly cash flow statements			
135.	Ages of inventories			
N.	**General Operations:**			
136.	Manual of Operations and Business process			
137.	Monthly Operations review Meeting			
138.	Profitability of the store			
139.	Competition/market price			
140.	Researching the market			

	Activity	D	F	E
141.	Fixed prices			
142.	Critical role of buyers			
143.	Walk the floors			
144.	Timeliness in innovation and logistics			
145.	Customer complaints and suggestions statement			
146.	Price tags to underscore branding			
O.	**Retail is People:**			
147.	Organisation Chart			
148.	Number of Staff			
149.	Budgeting for staff			
150.	Job descriptions and specifications			
151.	Gender in recruitment			
152.	Countries of origin			
153.	Formulation of relevant tests			
154.	Formation of recruitment team			
155.	Schedule of recruitment			
156.	Administrative arrangements			
157.	Arrival and housing arrangements			
158.	Transport arrangements			
P.	**Staff and Service:**			
159.	Grooming			
160.	Uniforms of staff			
161.	Frequency of washing			
162.	Treatment of women/girls			
163.	Language skills			
164.	Drinking water and beverages			
165.	Shoe shine arrangements			
166.	Best word: Smile			
167.	First Aid Boxes			
168.	Refrigerator and microwave			

Activity		D	F	E
169.	Daily morning meetings			
170.	Customer management skills			
171.	Training and development			
172.	Operating floor rules/Disciplinary situations			
173.	Theft, pilferage, shrinkages issues/responsibilities			
174.	Lockers for staff			
175.	Staff meal timings			
176.	Staff eating areas			
177.	Staff recreation area/room			
178.	Staff discounts permitted			
179.	Quiet room			
Q.	**Targets and Incentives:**			
180.	Monthly/quarterly targets			
181.	System of incentives			
182.	Communication of targets/incentives			
183.	Transparency in incentives			
184.	Weekly, fortnightly review of target achievement			
185.	Responsibility for administration			
R.	**Training and Development:**			
186.	Areas of Training			
187.	Focus: customer service and technical knowledge			
188.	Number of participants			
189.	Survey of external agencies			
190.	Selection of agency			
191.	Involve suppliers for technical inputs			
192.	Feedback from participants			

Activity	D	F	E
S. Cash Collections:			
193. Policy cash, credit, cheques			
194. Responsibility for cash			
195. Daily cash collections: reconciliation			
196. Overnight safe keeping			
197. Shortages, reporting, issues			
198. Cash memo records			
199. Deposits in banks etc./frequency/responsibility			
200. Insurance			
T. Security in Store:			
201. Number of entrances, exits in store			
202. Number of guards required and positioning			
203. Number of cameras			
204. Room for CCTV monitors			
205. Room for guards			
206. Connection to monitors in office			
U. Equipment Maintenance:			
207. List of equipment with details/dates			
208. Maintenance frequency, schedule and records			
209. Painting maintenance			
210. Replacements/repairs budgets, responsibilities			
V. Warehouses and Backrooms:			
211. Purpose of warehouses			
212. Requirements of space based on lead delivery periods etc.			
213. Visibility			

Activity	D	F	E
214. Flooring to handle movement of trolleys etc.			
215. Fitments and racks			
216. Trolleys			
217. Locks – keys, responsibilities			
218. Loading, unloading bays			
219. Cleanliness and orderliness			
W. Rest Rooms:			
220. Restrooms Management			
221. Separate facilities for men and women			
222. Cleaning schedule			
223. Cleaning materials			
224. Ventilation arrangements			
225. Hand drying machines/Disposable tissues			
226. Space for advertising			
X. Launch of Store:			
227. Objectives of the launch			
228. Finalisation of advertising agency			
229. Finalisation of Events Management Agency			
230. Media launch i.e. press, television radio, etc.			
231. Outdoor media			
232. Campaign periods			
233. List of activities			
234. Budgets			
235. Date of launch			
236. Co-ordinate with Mall management			
237. Invites			
238. Celebrity Inauguration			
239. Launch function			
240. Briefing of staff			

Activity	D	F	E
241. Greeters			
242. Press Conference			
243. Refreshments for customers, staff			
244. Incentives, free gifts to consumers, staff			
245. Gifts, balloons for kids, etc.			
246. Show for kids: face painting, painting etc.			
247. Anticipate and factor competition reactions			
248. Repeat advertising			
249. Payments to all vendors			
250. Thanks mails			
251. Calibrating results			
Y. Marketing and Promotion: Post Launch			
252. Marketing and Promotions			
253. Vendor participation			
254. Festival offers			
Z. Strategic E-Commerce Initiatives:			
255. Online sales etc.			
256. Social media and digital marketing			
257. Take Your Breath away			
258. Rejoice			

By Hari Chand Aneja
Available on Amazon

By Hari Chand Aneja
Available on Amazon

**Also by Rajendra K. Aneja
Available on Amazon**

Also by Rajendra K. Aneja
Available on Amazon

Also by Rajendra K. Aneja
Available on Amazon

Also by Rajendra K. Aneja
Available on Amazon

MY EXPERIENCES IN MODERN RETAIL

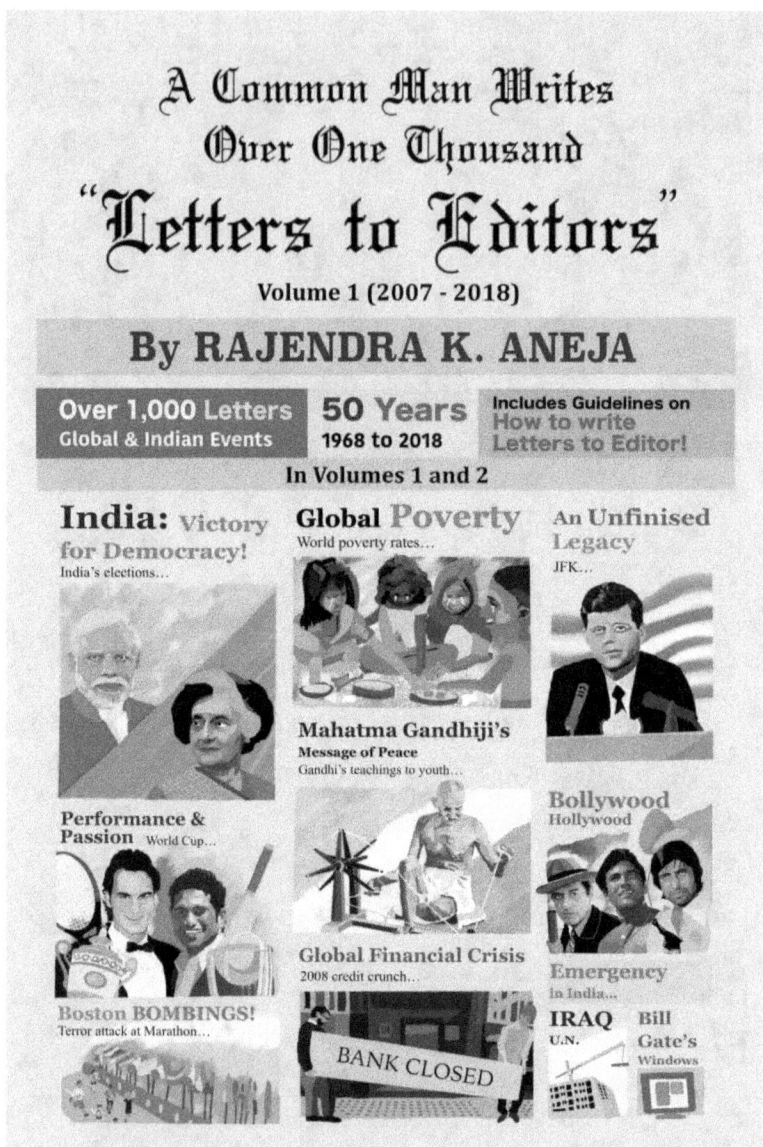

Also by Rajendra K. Aneja
Available on Amazon

Also by Rajendra K. Aneja

Available on Amazon

Also by Rajendra K. Aneja
Available on Amazon

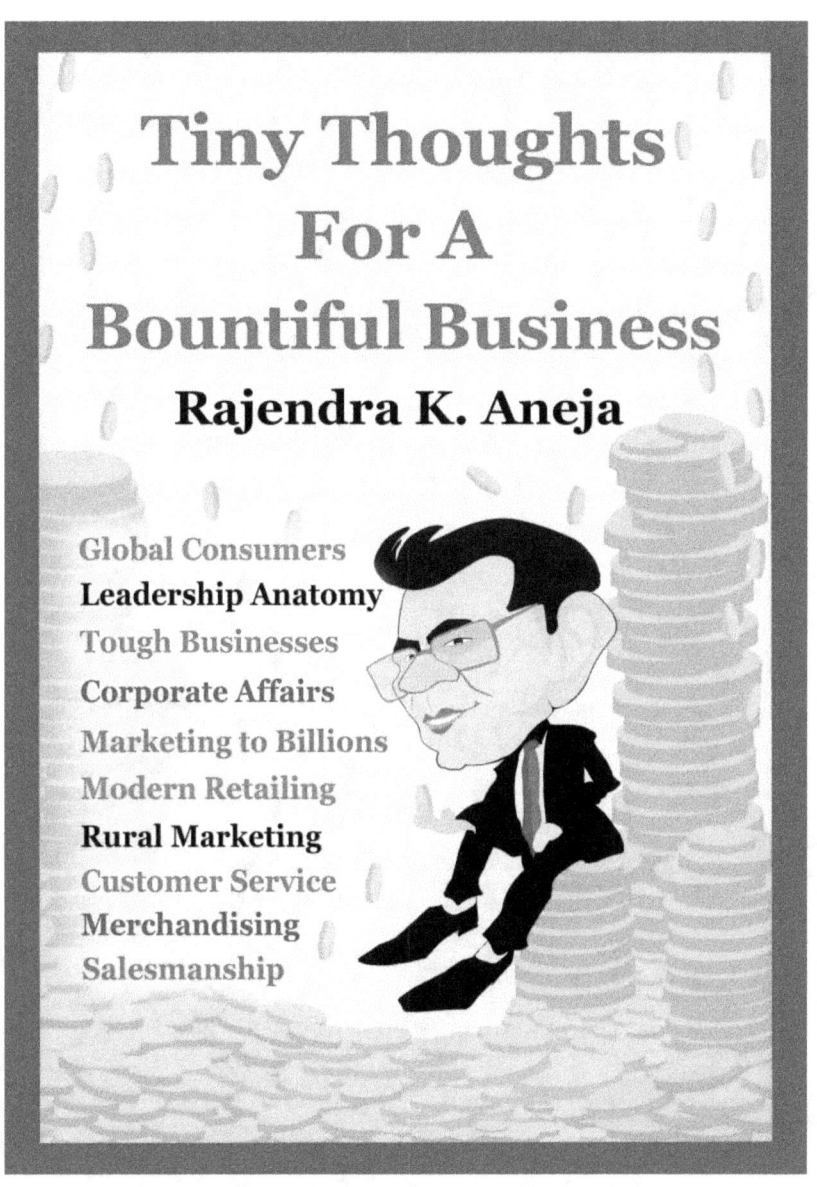

Also by Rajendra K. Aneja
Available on Amazon

www.ingramcontent.com/pod-product-compliance
Lightning Source LLC
Chambersburg PA
CBHW070624220526
45466CB00001B/88